Dedicated to my family: Crystal Rae, Marco Aurelo, Amaia Fae, and Felix Caius.

Published by Panta Rhei

www.pantarhei.media

Copy Editor: Christian de Quincey

Contents

Some think that the soul pervades the whole universe, whence perhaps came Thales's view that everything is full of gods

—Aristotle

INTRODUCTION

After graduating from college, like many recent graduates, I was unsure of myself and the direction in which I should take my life. I had a job which I enjoyed, but I found myself questioning exactly what the purpose of my life should be.

In order to clarify my thoughts, I decided to write a book on the purpose of life. Perhaps that was a little presumptuous for a twenty-one-year-old fresh out of school, but I felt that if I couldn't pick a goal that I could somehow justify, what hope was there that I wouldn't waste my life?

I wrote a one-page outline, detailing what I believed the purpose of life to be and the proper way I should organize my life and goals in order to achieve that purpose. The outline was broken up into various sub-topics which I then began to study in-depth in order to be able to write a proper book.

I began a systematic study of science, Christianity, Buddhism and philosophy in order to flesh out the hazy ideas floating in my mind. When I encountered Stoicism, Epicureanism and the works of Spinoza and Whitehead, my life was forever changed. As I began to read, I notice that I had to make some small changes to my outline. The more I read, the more I was forced to change it. After a while, I stopped making changes. I was in such a state of confusion that I was well beyond the point of simply editing and tweaking my original idea of the purpose of life. I wasn't even sure I could start over with a new version, I was truly perplexed.

The first problem I encountered was the problem of pain. If God loves us, why does he allow pain? Perhaps life is a test, I reasoned. But it seemed very cruel for a supposedly omnipotent being to create a universe full of pain and misery and throw sentient beings into it to see how they do. Surely, God couldn't be like that, I thought. And if He was, then I had no hope of being able to understand Him.

It was through contemplating this and many other similar problems that I began to feel that God could not be something separate from us. God must experience what we experience. God is not watching us, He is living through us. The very concept of a God as some sort of separate person, some sort of 'He' apart from us, began to feel more and more indefensible. If I felt it was cruel for me personally to put someone in pain, how could I justify a super-being who allows all of the famines, wars and disasters I saw around me and in history?

This led me to a period of atheism, until the logical inconsistencies of scientific materialism and dualism became too much for me to handle.

When I began my studies, my very idea of philosophy reflected my idea of the nature of reality. The world to me seemed largely dead and only sparsely inhabited by life. Likewise, philosophy was dead. It was a theoretical, intellectual construct. It was a purely rational investigation of nature, a systematic categorization of reality.

But as I progressed, the world came alive. I began to see life everywhere, nothing was dead, nothing was still. Everything was in motion. Everything was full of mind and life. Philosophy likewise came alive for me and it became a way of life. It became something I turned to every day to guide my interactions with others, control my passions and provide meaning to my life.

Philosophy has been indispensable to me in dealing with the challenges I've faced over the years. As I slowly developed a more systematic worldview and understanding of the nature of things, I found myself more and more at peace with myself and the world around me.

The book I have written is completely different from the book I set out to write more than 15 years ago. Many of my conclusions I reach are the exact opposite of what I believed when I started. This book is an attempt at a more precise depiction of the nature of reality and what that means for how I should live my life. This book is itself a spiritual exercise. In writing it, in the repetitive practice of expressing my beliefs on paper, in my various attempts to express the same things in different ways, I instruct myself.

I have given up attempting explanations of the ultimate nature of reality, accurate observations are difficult enough. I do not believe certain questions can be answered. We will never know why the universe exists and why it is the way it is. But a better understanding of the true nature of things can have very practical effects on our daily lives. *-Rodrigo Etcheto, Olympia, Washington 2018*

How to use this book

It may seem obvious, but I'd like to explain the frame of mind that I think will help you the most when reading this book.

Ancient vs Modern Philosophy

Our modern idea of philosophy is wrong. We see philosophy as dry and academic, as the exposition of abstruse theoretical systems of thought that have absolutely no application in daily life. Philosophy today is dead and lifeless.

That's not what philosophy was in the ancient world...

My Biggest Discovery

When I first started studying ancient philosophy, I quickly realized that those philosophers weren't just talking about abstract, academic theories in the way we think of philosophy today. To the ancients, ***philosophy was a way of life***.

What exactly does that mean? To be philosopher didn't mean to be an academic or teacher. It didn't mean to be someone that develops theories. In the past, many philosophers didn't develop any theories at all, never taught and never did any formal schooling. They simply lived a 'philosophical' lifestyle.

Their lifestyle set them apart from everyone else. They lived simply, modestly and as much as possible in a state of deep thought. One of the ways they did this was through regular spiritual exercises.

The ancient philosophers practiced a variety of spiritual exercises which today we would recognize as a form of active meditation. They would explore certain topics and ideas that were important to understanding the cosmos and remaining in the proper philosophical frame of mind. They would do this through spoken dialogues with others; in other words, actual conversations with other philosophers in which they would explore the nuances of philosophical concepts. They would also have internal dialogues with themselves, read regularly, write to themselves, engage in acts of the imagination to change their perspective and expand their world-view and they would explore the natural world to learn as much as possible about the true nature of things.

In order to gain the most from this book, you need to see this as one large spiritual exercise that you can embark on alongside me. I wrote it in bite-sized pieces because each idea is a topic for meditation, an idea to explore over and over until it becomes something you feel in your bones, deep inside you.

The goal of this book is to show you the intellectual journey that I went through to find a deeper meaning in my life and put myself at peace with my existence. These are the questions I posed to myself and the active meditations I performed (and still do in some way, every day).

This is the chain of ideas I discovered which helped me learn to live a more 'philosophical' life: a life not dedicated to external pursuits, but to the internal pursuit of developing my mind, improving my character and becoming a better person.

I learned these lessons (and am still learning them...) over years of struggle with self-doubt, confusion, financial stress, bankruptcy, eviction and medical crises. I suffered from an existential crisis for a long time, not knowing who I was or where I should go.

Spiritual Exercises

Each idea in here is presented several times, first in simple short forms then in more detailed forms and finally in the shortest forms possible.

Each concept is intended as a topic for contemplation and meditation. Many practitioners of mindfulness meditation like to make their minds 'empty'. This is obviously an excellent practice, but I find that mindfulness which actively probes into the nature of reality to be just as inspiring and uplifting. By using your mind as a 'beam of light', you can peer deep into the things that surround you.

I have avoided difficult academic language as much as possible. In order for something to be of practical use, it must be easily understood and remembered.

Repetition is key. I've found that I have to repeat these ideas over and over to myself, contemplate them, meditate on them and formulate them for myself over and over. As Epictetus said, these ideas must be 'at hand' always, so you can turn to them when you need them.

The best way to do that is to have a dialogue with yourself, write to yourself, find the way of expressing these ideas to yourself so that they are embedded deep in your mind.

I find that one of the best ways for me to truly learn something is to imagine I am explaining it to someone else. When I go on my photographic excursions, I typically walk through a forest, debating myself within my own head. My wife says she can see me talking to myself, silently moving my lips and waving my hands. I must look crazy!

But this is how I probe my thoughts for weakness, gaps and inconsistencies. This is how I make these ideas concrete, repeatable, and always 'at hand'.

Photography

Finally, I should explain the photography you'll find throughout this book. All are my original works, except for the mummy portrait (I wish I could see that in real life to take a portrait!).

One of my favorite forms of active meditation is to go on excursions in the forests, mountains and coastline of my home, the Pacific Northwest.

When I first started doing this, as I was hiking and contemplating things, I would come across a beautiful scene and snap a picture with my phone. Well...you can see where this eventually took me. Soon enough, the cell phone wasn't enough and I started upgrading to better and better 'real' cameras.

Before I knew it, I was going out with professional gear, and photographing in a serious way. I found that I could express certain philosophical concepts through imagery, as well as words. The photographs would capture the idea and help remind me of a concept. Photographs made concepts more 'real'. The images helped make those ideas have greater impact and served as reminders. From there my passion for photographing nature grew and grew.

Daily Practice

Although it's difficult to do this sort of practice daily, when I do, I find myself in a totally different frame of mind and better able to deal with the every day problems of life. I can change my perspective and observe life through the viewpoint of the cosmos.

I find I have the most luck when I set up triggers to remind me to meditate. For example, I have certain photographs and images that remind me of a concept and spur me to spend some time in contemplation.

Whenever I can, nothing beats a hike in the forest. When I have time I love to go out in the morning and spend some time walking and thinking. I find the rest of the day to have a different sort of energy from a normal day.

Other times, I simply leave a book by my nightstand so every night before I go to bed I see it and feel guilty if I don't read a little. Reading and re-reading classic works serves to reinforce the concepts and make them sink in.

Finally, I find writing and re-writing to be extremely effective for me. I keep a journal hidden away that I occassionally pick up and write in. But most importantly, I keep a note-taking app on my phone and jot down ideas and formulations as often as I can.

Get in Touch

If you have any questions, comments or would just like to say hi, please feel free to get in touch with me at:

hello@everythingisfullofgods.com

or on any of the usual social media tools (just search for Everything is Full of Gods and you should be able to find me)

I'd genuinely love to hear from you!

To see more of my photography go to:

www.everythingisfullofgods.com

everything —

— is full of gods

When Antisthenes was asked what profit he had derived from philosophy he replied: "The ability to converse with myself".

-Diogenes Laertius

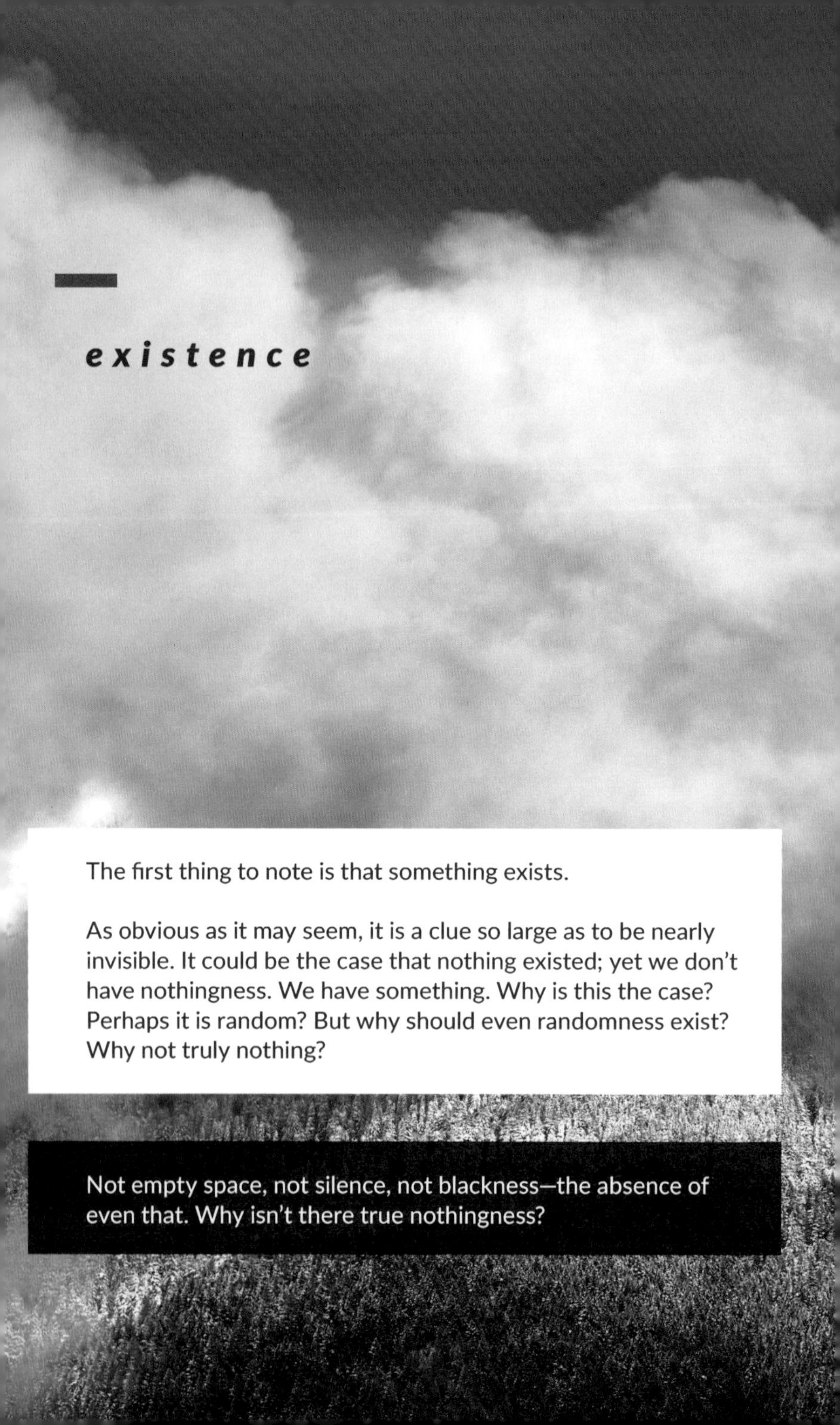

existence

The first thing to note is that something exists.

As obvious as it may seem, it is a clue so large as to be nearly invisible. It could be the case that nothing existed; yet we don't have nothingness. We have something. Why is this the case? Perhaps it is random? But why should even randomness exist? Why not truly nothing?

Not empty space, not silence, not blackness—the absence of even that. Why isn't there true nothingness?

The fact that something exists seems inexplicable by religion, science or anything. It is a brute fact. If the universe is here because God created it, why does God exist? If the universe exists because the laws of nature created it, why do the laws of nature exist? Why not nothing? Truly nothing? No God, no Big Bang, no natural laws, no randomness, no truth, no logic. Not even the abstract fact of 2+2=4.

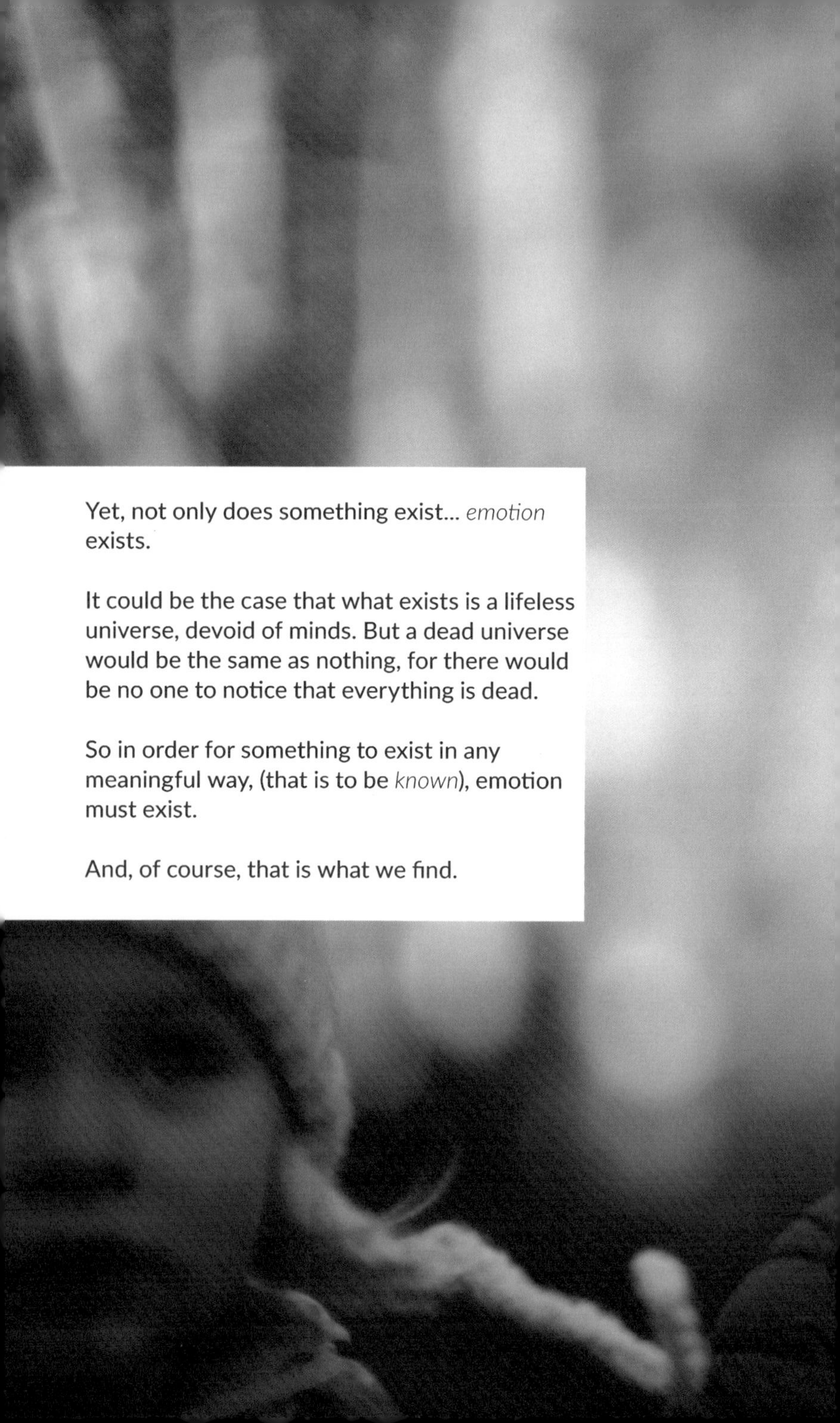

Yet, not only does something exist... *emotion* exists.

It could be the case that what exists is a lifeless universe, devoid of minds. But a dead universe would be the same as nothing, for there would be no one to notice that everything is dead.

So in order for something to exist in any meaningful way, (that is to be *known*), emotion must exist.

And, of course, that is what we find.

one thing
or
two things?

What exists in the universe? One kind of stuff or two kinds of stuff?

If there's just one kind of stuff, physical stuff, then we can explain atoms, molecules, chairs and mountains. Physical things exist and obey the laws of nature we know through science.

But how do we explain thinking things? Are there two kinds of stuff: physical and mental? Would this explain humans and our thoughts, feelings, and emotions? Perhaps we are combinations of physical stuff and mental stuff? It certainly seems that way: We have bodies (physical) and minds (mental).

The modern view claims that physical things like atoms have no mental properties. More complicated things made from many atoms therefore have no mental properties either. A chair is just a bunch of atoms, it doesn't think. But how to explain animals, especially humans?

We are also made from many supposedly unthinking atoms. Yet we think. Where do our minds come from? If each atom has absolutely no mental properties, absolutely no emotions, then how can adding together billions of them all of a sudden conjure up the joys of watching a sunrise or the taste of apple pie? If one atom has no mind, then presumably ten atoms have no mind, and 1,000 atoms have no mind. But, according to modern science and philosophy, somewhere along the line, when organisms evolved to many billions and billions of atoms, a mind suddenly appeared. How? How can you go from absolute zero, to even the smallest infinitesimal bit of anything?

The leap from nothing—from absolutely no mental properties whatsoever—to even the smallest flicker of a sensation or emotion would be the most radical break in all of the natural world. Nowhere else do we see breaks like this, everywhere else in nature and in evolution things happen gradually, from something that already exists. If purely physical stuff cannot account for the existence of minds, perhaps we need a second kind of stuff in the universe—mental stuff. Some things, such as chairs, are made just from physical stuff. But some things, such as people and other animals, are made from combinations of physical and mental stuff.

According to this view, physical things have no mental properties and mental things have no physical properties. Thoughts, for example, don't weigh anything, nor can you hit them with a tennis racket. But if this is true, then how could physical and mental stuff come together to interact? How could two things with no shared attributes possibly influence each other? If the brain were purely physical, how could it possibly influence or respond to a non-physical mind? Such interaction would be impossible. The idea that mind and brain are two different and separate things, therefore, fails to account for the obvious mind-body interactions each of us experiences routinely.

We all know from personal experience that our bodies affect our minds and our minds affect our bodies. Somehow, they do interact. Perhaps, then, brains and minds have a different kind of relationship? Maybe they don't exist in parallel; but, instead, one arises, or "emerges," from the other?

For example, perhaps mind emerges from mindless brain cells. Perhaps the sheer complexity of our brains is enough to produce or create our minds?

But this raises a different problem: How can one thing emerge from another thing with which it has nothing in common? For the mind to emerge from the brain, something physical must produce something non-physical. This would not be emergence, this would be magic. How could physical things possibly create non-physical things?

Believing in two types of things, physical and mental, leaves us unable to explain how they interact. Believing in purely physical things leaves us unable to explain the mind. So we are left with a final option: There's one type of stuff, but it isn't purely physical. Rather, this stuff has a physical and a mental aspect. All things are made this same stuff. One does not create the other, because there is no other; they both exist at the bottom of everything.

the nature of the physical

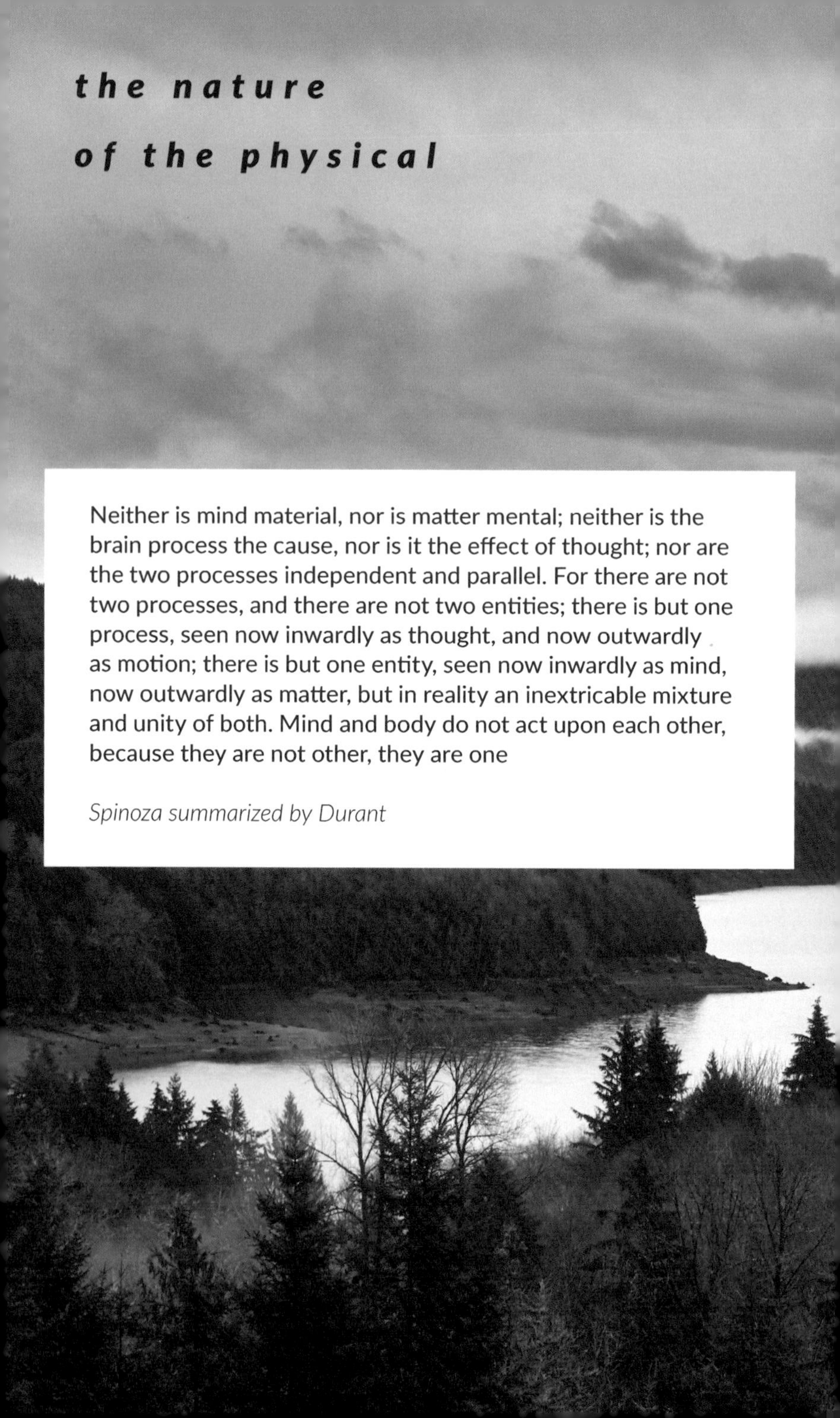

Neither is mind material, nor is matter mental; neither is the brain process the cause, nor is it the effect of thought; nor are the two processes independent and parallel. For there are not two processes, and there are not two entities; there is but one process, seen now inwardly as thought, and now outwardly as motion; there is but one entity, seen now inwardly as mind, now outwardly as matter, but in reality an inextricable mixture and unity of both. Mind and body do not act upon each other, because they are not other, they are one

Spinoza summarized by Durant

thoughts & actions

Here's another way to think about the problem of how mind and body interact: Ask yourself whether your thoughts cause your actions. We're accustomed to speaking as if mind and body are different things, but is this really the case? Common sense tells us that mind and body influence each other, but are not separate. If they actually were two separate and different things, it's difficult to see how they could possibly interact.

Imagine you are sitting in a chair and suddenly feel thirsty and decide you want a glass of water. You stand up to get it. What caused you to get up? Was it the desire for water? But what is that desire? Is it a physical thing? Is it made of atoms? If it is, how come no one has ever been able to capture the atoms of a feeling, desire or emotion, put them in a glass jar and weigh them? If the desire itself is a physical thing, it must be made of atoms or some kind of physical particle. In that case, we should be able to detect and measure it. Yet this has never happened. But if the desire is not a physical thing, not made of atoms, if it is instead a mental thing, then how could that non-physical desire possibly make physical muscles in your body move? The nerves in your muscle are physical, and so only other physical things can interact with them. This problem of interaction is fatal to the idea of two separate types of stuff in the universe.

It is more likely that instead of two things interacting, there is only one process occurring. From the inside we feel it as thought, from the outside it appears as action.

what am I made of?

My mind is real. I know this because I feel my mind directly. It's the only thing I directly experience. It is me.

My body is also real. Unlike my mind, however, I don't know this directly. I don't directly experience my body except through my mind. But I believe my body is real, rationally and intuitively, because to believe that my mind is somehow floating in nothingness, unanchored to my body or anything else seems silly. Thus, the rest of the physical universe is also real and I am embedded in it.

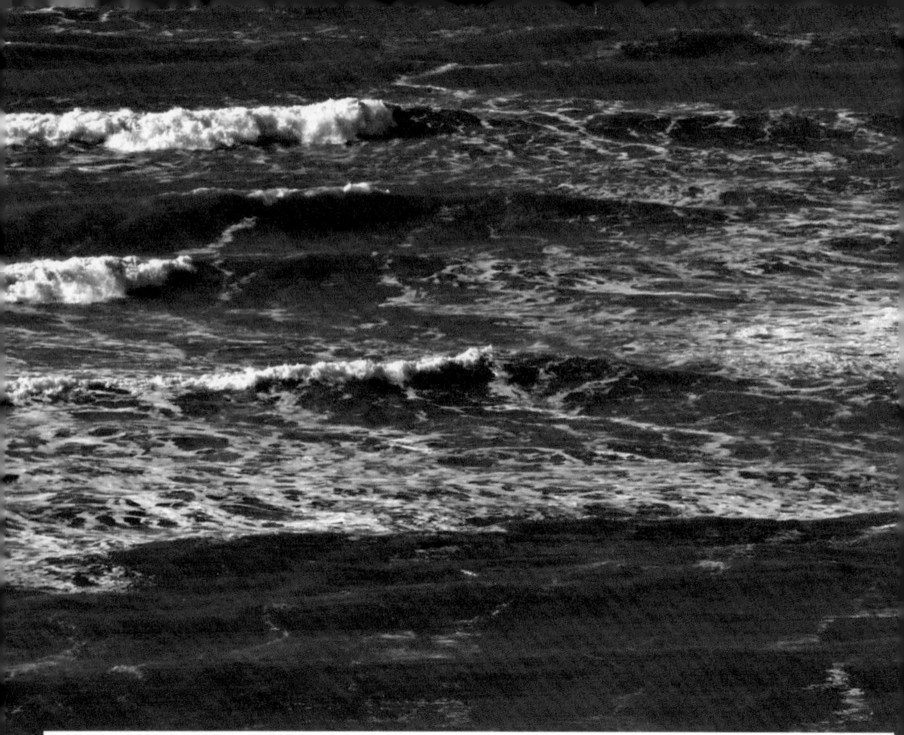

So what am I made of?

There is both a mental and a physical aspect to my existence. I am a thinking thing. Am I unique in the universe? That also seems silly. My nature must be universal. I must be like everything else and everything else must be like me in a fundamental sense. It would be too much of a coincidence for me to be made of the only stuff that can think. It can't be that only the matter that makes it into my brain is capable of thought. All matter must be similar to the matter that composes me and my brain, and the matter of my body must be similar to all other matter.

Because I know I have experiences, thoughts, and emotions, then any description of the universe that leaves that out must be incomplete. Physics, therefore, must be incomplete. After all, wouldn't it be strange if I cannot be described purely in mechanistic terms, but the rest of the universe could be?

Since my mentality is fundamentally connected to my physicality, and I am not a unique thing (everything is made of the same kind of stuff), all matter must, in some form, have a mental aspect.

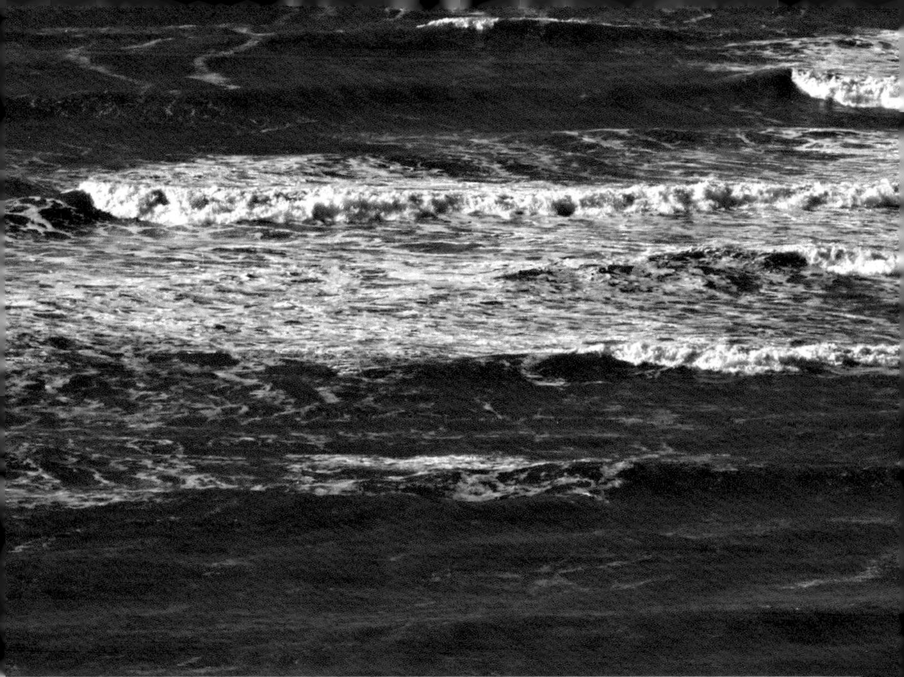

The stuff of my body does not simply exist, statically. It is in constant flux. My body is made up of some 10 trillion of my own cells and another 100 trillion bacterial cells. But my cells are in a constant state of decay and repair. Every day, ten billion die and are replaced. The average age of a cell in my body is seven to ten years old and many live much briefer lives than that. The cells lining my stomach last only five days. Red blood cells travel 1,000 miles through my circulatory system in a short 120 days before being destroyed in the spleen. The cells that make up the surface layer of the skin are replaced every two weeks. My liver is completely replaced every 300 to 500 days. Even bones, which seem so tough and permanent, are in a constant state of decay and repair. My entire skeleton is replaced every ten years or so. The neurons that make up my brain likewise have a lifespan shorter than “me.” Some neurons truly appear to last my whole lifetime while others break down and need to be replaced. Neurons in the cerebral cortex are especially important for forming memories, but they also die and are replaced throughout my life. Their exact lifespan is still unknown but estimated to be roughly twenty years. And even further down, the atoms and molecules that make up those cells are not static things. They are bits of energy in constant flux.

So what exactly am I? Am I the cells that make up my body today? What about the cells that made up my body ten years ago? Who was that? Am I the atoms that make up my body today? How many times have these atoms already been replaced?

I've already died many times in my life. The "me" when I was five years old is gone forever. The "me" from even ten years ago is probably totally different from the "me" today, at least physically. Who will I be in the future? I'll keep continuously dying and being reborn, until one day my metabolism stops repairing my cells, the rebirth stops, and I die one last time, but this time permanently.

I am like a vortex of matter, a temporary form created from the stuff of my surrounding environment. A knot in the fabric of the universe, unique in the ever-changing pattern I create through time, yet made of the same stuff as everything else.

commonsense, intuition & absurdity

What can we use to guide our thinking? Many of our commonsense notions turn out to be false. We could easily believe the world to be flat. After all, this is what we see with our own eyes; yet now we know that's not actually the case. Commonsense comes to us through culture, and can often change with new scientific developments.

However, one type of commonsense cannot be revised without the risk of falling into absurdity. These "elemental commonsense notions" are presupposed by all of us in our daily lives, including by scientists in their pursuit of science:

Elemental Commonsense Notions

-Our minds are real: we feel them directly and unlike the idea of a flat Earth, in this we cannot be mistaken.

-The external world is also real and our minds are inseparable from the physical universe.

-The regularity we experience of the physical world affecting our mental lives, and our mental lives affecting the physical world, is so consistent that to believe it is all a figment of our imaginations would be absurd.

-Time is real: we feel its passage directly, our feelings are never still.

-We are free and choose among genuine alternatives through the deliberative power of our minds.

-Our bodies act on our minds and our minds act on our bodies.

-Abstract norms—such as beauty, truth and justice—are real: we may disagree on exactly what each one is, but that there are such things no one disputes. Even if these may be creations of our minds, the reality of the mental immediately makes these abstractions real, as well.

Because of the incredible success of science, many scientific arguments seem rational, at least at first. But when you think through their logical implications the end result can be so absurd the argument collapses in on itself.

For example, according to the standard physicalist view, because atoms are purely physical, the brain creates the mind, but the mind doesn't act on the brain or body. The mind, then, appears like a vapor that evaporates from the brain, creating emotions but little else. But think through what this implies and what else we're forced to believe if we choose to believe this. We would have to believe that evolution created emotions from a universe that had absolutely no emotion. In other words, there would have been a point in the history of the universe when not a single mind, no emotion, existed. Then, suddenly, the first emotion, however small, happened.

In this scenario, we would have to believe that as animals evolved, eventually an animal was born with a brain structure complex enough to have the universe's first mind. At some point in history, this animal would have appeared, born to a mother with no mind.

Yet nowhere else in nature do we see a radical break like this, where something gets created from nothing. Everything in nature gradually changes from one thing to the next. This change occurs at varying speeds, but it is **change**—never creation out of nothing.

Take, for example, the idea that mind evolved from mindless matter. Once the first mind somehow evolved, how could it possibly have given its possessor a survival advantage? If mind can't affect the body, regardless of what the mind thinks, it would have no effect on the animal, and, therefore, would not change its ability to survive.

We would have to further believe that the thoughts you're having right now can't influence the thoughts you will have in a moment. Since thoughts can't influence the brain, the next physical brain state you enter will have nothing to do with your current thoughts. Nor have your past thoughts influenced who you are right now. The whole time you thought you had an inner mental life, it was just atoms banging around in your brain, obeying only the laws of physics and ignoring your thoughts completely.

According to this argument, your next thoughts will come about purely because of the physical activity of the neural states you're in right now. This physical activity is completely predetermined by the laws of physics. Indeed, this very argument about the absurdity of minds not affecting brains was predetermined from the beginning of time, including whether you agree with it or not.

This result is so nonsensical the argument must involve a false assumption somewhere. And, of course, it does: our minds do affect our bodies just like our bodies affect our minds. This mistake happens because we don't truly understand the nature of the physical. Although the starting premise of the standard scientific view—that atoms are purely physical—might seem rational and backed up by much evidence, its logical conclusions are so ludicrous we must be making an error—not recognizing that mentality is part of physicality. At the root of everything, whatever the fundamental particles of the universe turn out to be, we will find a physical aspect and a mental aspect. From these fundamental particles, complex structures gradually evolve. Some of these slowly exhibit more freedom and more thinking, until animals as complex as humans or cetaceans arrive.

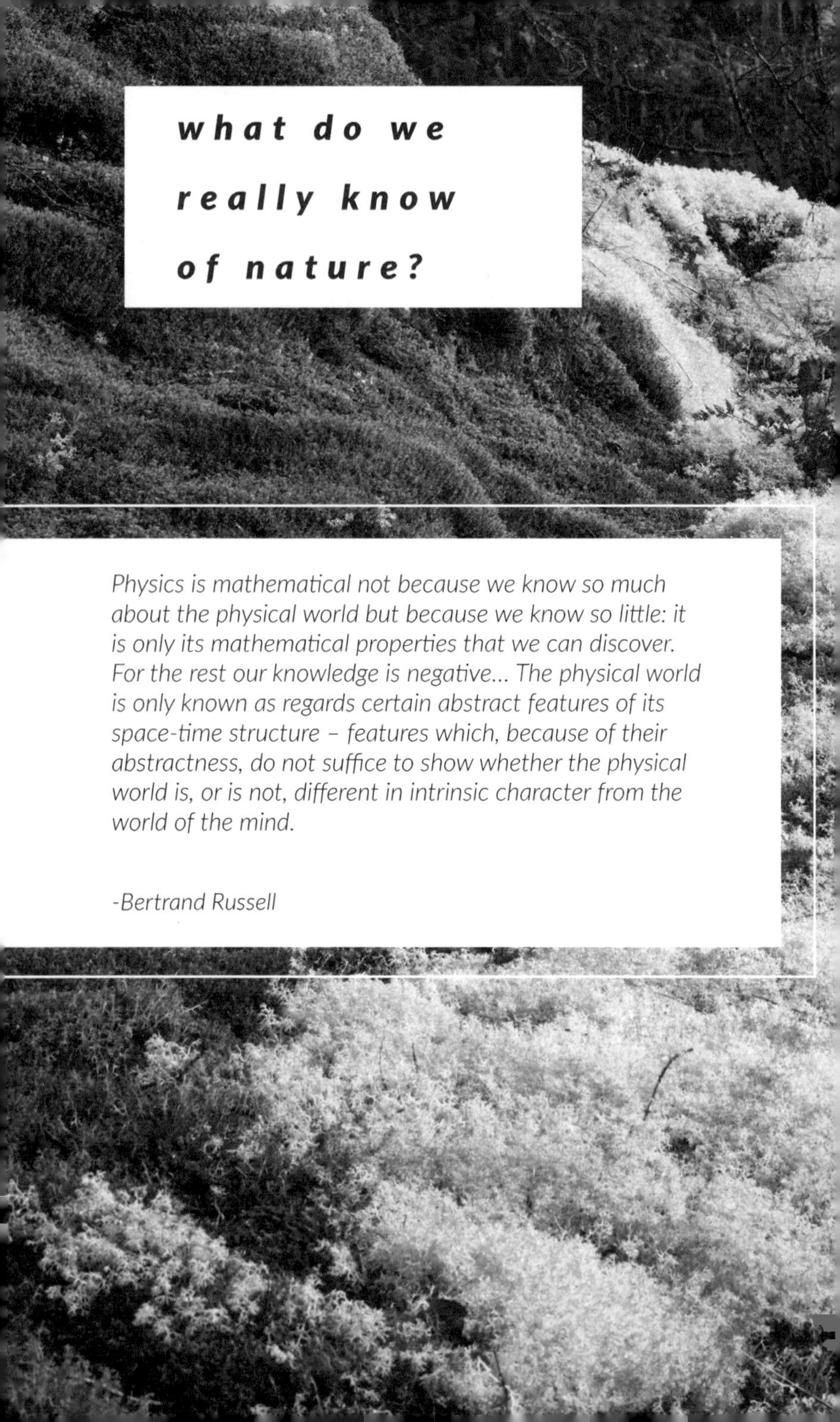

what do we really know of nature?

Physics is mathematical not because we know so much about the physical world but because we know so little: it is only its mathematical properties that we can discover. For the rest our knowledge is negative... The physical world is only known as regards certain abstract features of its space-time structure – features which, because of their abstractness, do not suffice to show whether the physical world is, or is not, different in intrinsic character from the world of the mind.

-Bertrand Russell

The recognition that our knowledge of the nature of the objects treated in physics consists solely of readings of pointers [on instrument dials] and other indicators transforms our view of the status of physical knowledge in a fundamental way... How can this collection of ordinary knowledge be a thinking machine? But what knowledge have we of the nature of atoms that renders it at all incongruous that they should constitute a thinking object? ... science has nothing to say as to the intrinsic nature of the atom....

The atom is, like everything else in physics, a schedule of pointer readings [on instruments dials]. The schedule is, we agree, attached to some unknown background. Why not then attach it to something of a spiritual [ie mental] nature of which a prominent characteristic is thought. It seems rather silly to attach it to something of a so-called concrete nature inconsistent with thought, and then to wonder where that thought comes from.

We have dismissed all preconception as to the background of our pointer readings, and for the most part can discover nothing as to its nature. But in one case – namely, for the pointer readings of my own brain – I have an insight which is not limited to the evidence of the pointer readings. That insight shows that they are attached to a background of consciousness.

-Sir Arthur Eddington

Nothing is so productive of greatness of mind as the ability to examine systematically and truthfully each thing we encounter in life, and to see these things in such a way as to comprehend the nature of the Cosmos, and what sort of benefits such things possess for both the Whole and for humans...This thing or circumstance that now gives me an impression: What is it? What is it made of? How long will it last? And, most important, what quality does it require of me, such as gentleness, courage, honesty, faith, simplicity, independence, and the like?

-Marcus Aurelius

the lack of a permanent self

I form a slowly changing pattern of activity in time, made up of rapidly changing parts. As water flows through a river, the water molecules that make up the river change from moment to moment, forming a river that slowly changes its own shape.

In a similar way, matter/mind is rapidly flowing through me. Or to be more precise, the flow itself is me. The pattern of activity that defines me meanders slowly through time. I look for my "self" in my mind and I don't find it. Moment by moment, new experiences happen and then they're gone. Nothing permanent resides in my mind, just a never-ending series of ever-changing perceptions. But who perceives my perceptions? No one. No little person lives in my brain, watching my experiences go by, like a man in a theater watching a movie. When I observe my own consciousness I never detect my self; I witness only the stream of sensations, thoughts, and emotions.

Unless I train my mind, I will grasp at those fleeting experiences as though they could be made permanent. These grasping impulses evolved for my survival, not my happiness. So I think and act as if I do have an unchanging self to preserve, and this grasping after impermanent experiences as if they were permanent leads to pain. A little bit of praise and my ego is inflated; but what is there to inflate? An insult and I am hurt. But what is there to hurt? My ephemeral mind perceives itself in this world and wants to find permanence where none exists.

My mind is real and in each moment, unified. I experience one single perspective of the universe each moment, but there is no single thing that is me.

We like to believe that some things have single causes. When our ancestors saw the sun, they imagined a chariot pulling it across the sky. But there's no one thing that causes the sun to move like that, just the combined gravitational pull of trillions and trillions of atoms.

Likewise, there's no one thing that is me. My mind is the unification of the mental aspect of billions and billions of fundamental particles.

the superorganism

How can your consciousness—a unified mental event—arise from many separate mental events? If the basic particles out of which everything is made each has a mental aspect, how can they all unite into a single, unified momentary consciousness? When it comes to the mind, analogies with physical phenomena are hopeless. Nevertheless, we must try.

In nature, we see examples of small fields adding up into big fields. For example, many small gravitational fields combine to form a large one. The mental aspect of the fundamental stuff must behave in a similar, cumulative way.

Consider ants. Each one behaves in a pretty simple way, yet together they form a superorganism: a colony. The colony behaves in much more complicated ways than any single ant, yet it's nothing more than thousands of ants put together. The colony influences the behavior of individual ants while at the same time each individual influences the behavior of the entire colony.

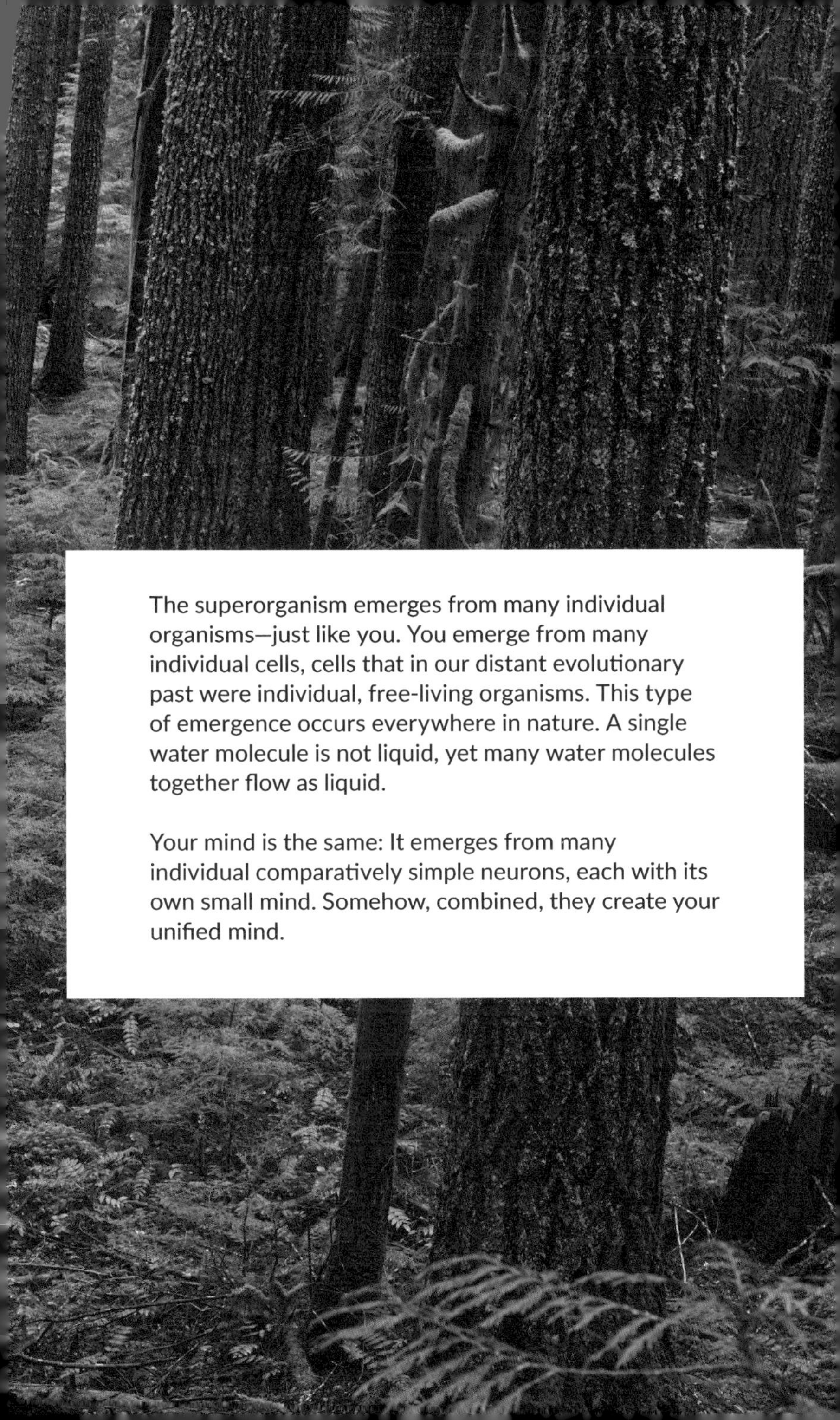

The superorganism emerges from many individual organisms—just like you. You emerge from many individual cells, cells that in our distant evolutionary past were individual, free-living organisms. This type of emergence occurs everywhere in nature. A single water molecule is not liquid, yet many water molecules together flow as liquid.

Your mind is the same: It emerges from many individual comparatively simple neurons, each with its own small mind. Somehow, combined, they create your unified mind.

other people's thoughts

We can reflect on our own experiences because we feel them directly. But how do you know that your friends have thoughts? You can't feel what they feel. If a friend cries, you assume she's sad. And if she laughs, you assume she's happy. But you don't really know she's sad; you just assume it based on her words and behavior. Unless you can somehow get inside her head and directly experience her emotions, you can't know for sure.

Isn't it possible that she's not feeling anything at all? For all you know, she's just going through the motions. Perhaps she's some sort of unfeeling zombie that acts exactly like a thinking, feeling human?

If you believe mind and brain are two things, then this zombie scenario becomes more plausible—because, according to this view, mind doesn't do anything. As long as the brain neurons fire correctly, you friend will behave the same as always. If for some reason something happened to her brain such that its neurons functioned as they always have, except for that last little bit that (presumably) creates consciousness, how could you ever tell? She would cry and the tears would flow, but inside her head there would be no mind and no feeling of sadness.

Or imagine a different universe. Imagine a universe exactly like this one, with the same natural laws, except the law that (some suppose) creates consciousness from physical neurons. In this alternative universe, everything works the same as it does here, except no one feels anything. But that doesn't matter! People in the alternative "zombie" universe would still get married; they would just never experience love. They might make art; but wouldn't feel beauty. Their brains would function exactly like ours, and therefore they would behave just as we do. Every natural law would be the same, except the one that's supposed to create minds from mindless physical atoms. All of the physical movements of the atoms in zombie brains would be the same as in ours and, therefore, the zombie behaviors would be the same.

In that alternative universe, no sense of redness or any other sensate quality, such as the warmth of heat, would ever be experienced. No experience of being alive would happen in Zombie World, which would consist exclusively of physical things bumping into each other. In that universe, animals just as complicated as us could evolve.

When we see a dangerous animal, electrochemical changes in our brains activate our muscles, enabling us to flee danger . . . and we feel fear. In the alternative universe, the same physical things, the same chemical changes, would happen. Muscles would contract and the zombie would flee . . . but without feeling any fear.

Clearly this is absurd. Without our feelings and emotions, our behavior would be impossible. No love and no art could exist without feeling. We flee dangerous animals because our muscles contract **and** because we feel fear. Our minds are not mere passengers in our bodies, just along for the ride. Our emotions do affect our behavior, so it can't be the case that if our emotions disappeared, our behavior would be unchanged. It is not the case that the world can be accurately described without emotional content. Despite what scientific materialism claims, physical activity in the brain does not depend only on other physical activity.

The physical and mental are so deeply intertwined in the fundamental stuff of the universe that one cannot exist without the other. The stuff of the universe is as much mind as it is matter.

We are not accidental, life is not an accident. Mind is not a side effect of physical activity or evolution. Our emotions are not flukes. Mind is central to the nature of physical reality. *Emotion is central to existence.*

With mind an intrinsic part of nature, then, evolution is not random or aimless—it has a goal, it is going somewhere.

If mind is everywhere, how can anything be mindless?

A good analogy may be gravity. We understand now that mass appears to warp the fabric of space-time, creating the gravitational fields we experience every day. In a similar way, brain matter must "warp" or affect its associated mind. Just as stars and massive planets create the largest gravitational fields, the complex interactions of the neurons of our brains would "warp" or influence the mental field. This warping of a background mental field that pervades all reality is what we experience as mental events. This claim has the further consequence that wherever matter exists mind or consciousness must be present, too. In this sense, *the entire universe must be conscious.*

Everything pulses with consciousness. This doesn't mean, of course, that everything is conscious in the same way a human is. After all, not everything has the same mass as a human either, why should everything have the same mental life as a human? But the ability to experience ***is*** fundamental to all matter, from the lowliest electron to the largest galaxy. This means the matter in our brains is no different from the matter in the rest of the universe. Complex human consciousness doesn't spring up out of nowhere in our brains; it builds up slowly from less complex minds already present in the electrons, atoms, and molecules that make up all of us.

As absurd as it might at first seem, the idea that matter everywhere possesses some trace of mentality turns out to be much more rational than the alternative of mindless matter in brains producing minds. Even rocks have some degree of mental life. The mental life of a human—with the concepts of past and future, self-consciousness, and complex emotions—requires a fully developed brain. But this doesn't mean that other things entirely lack experience. Like a two-sided coin, the universe consists of just a single kind of "stuff" that exhibits both physical and mental characteristics. This stuff has the physical properties that science tells us about and the mental properties we experience directly. From the "inside," matter is directly experienced as possessing feelings, thoughts, emotions, and choices. From the "outside," it is observed as action and movement. But all matter has the same fundamental properties.

does the universe have thoughts?

We imagine atoms moving through the void, but there really is no empty space with 'things' moving through it. What we perceive as individual things, or what we imagine as individual atoms, are knots in the fabric of space-time. They are like ripples on the surface of the sea. Everything is one interconnected system; separate, individual particles do not exist, just universal activity and wrinkles in the fabric of reality. This fabric is what everything is made of. As we know from our own experience, this "fabric" possesses physical and mental attributes—it feels. Therefore, the entire universe feels. What kind of feelings or emotions does it have? Who can tell?

Just because the universe's mind must be wholly unlike ours, does not mean it has no mind.

do things
exist for
an 'instant'?

Reality is not made of "things," but processes. There are no things. What we conceive of as atoms are composed of energy, constantly in flux. Processes are more fundamental than things. The ultimate stuff of reality is not a thing that could exist apart from time. Reality is always in process. All things exist in time.

Time and change are fundamental aspects of everything. Because of this, nothing could exist in an instant, by itself. Everything is in process, transition, and transformation. This means that for anything to exist it requires a minimum duration of time. Nothing exists apart from other processes or apart from time.

I take a breath; when do those molecules I've just inhaled become part of my body? I exhale; am I exhaling part of my body that now becomes part of the environment?

My brain requires a certain minimum amount of time with which to fire its neurons. My thoughts require a minimum amount of time to arise and pass. It takes even more time to make sure my thoughts are coherent. Nothing can be described without taking into account the time it takes to exist.

Experience constantly changes because its associated matter is constantly in flux. The unstoppable process of reality is constant change. Because of this, we continually have new experiences and cannot tie down a permanent self.

If I wasn't changing, I would be static and have no experience. To experience ***is*** to change. Likewise, the universe is constantly changing, constantly experiencing new things.

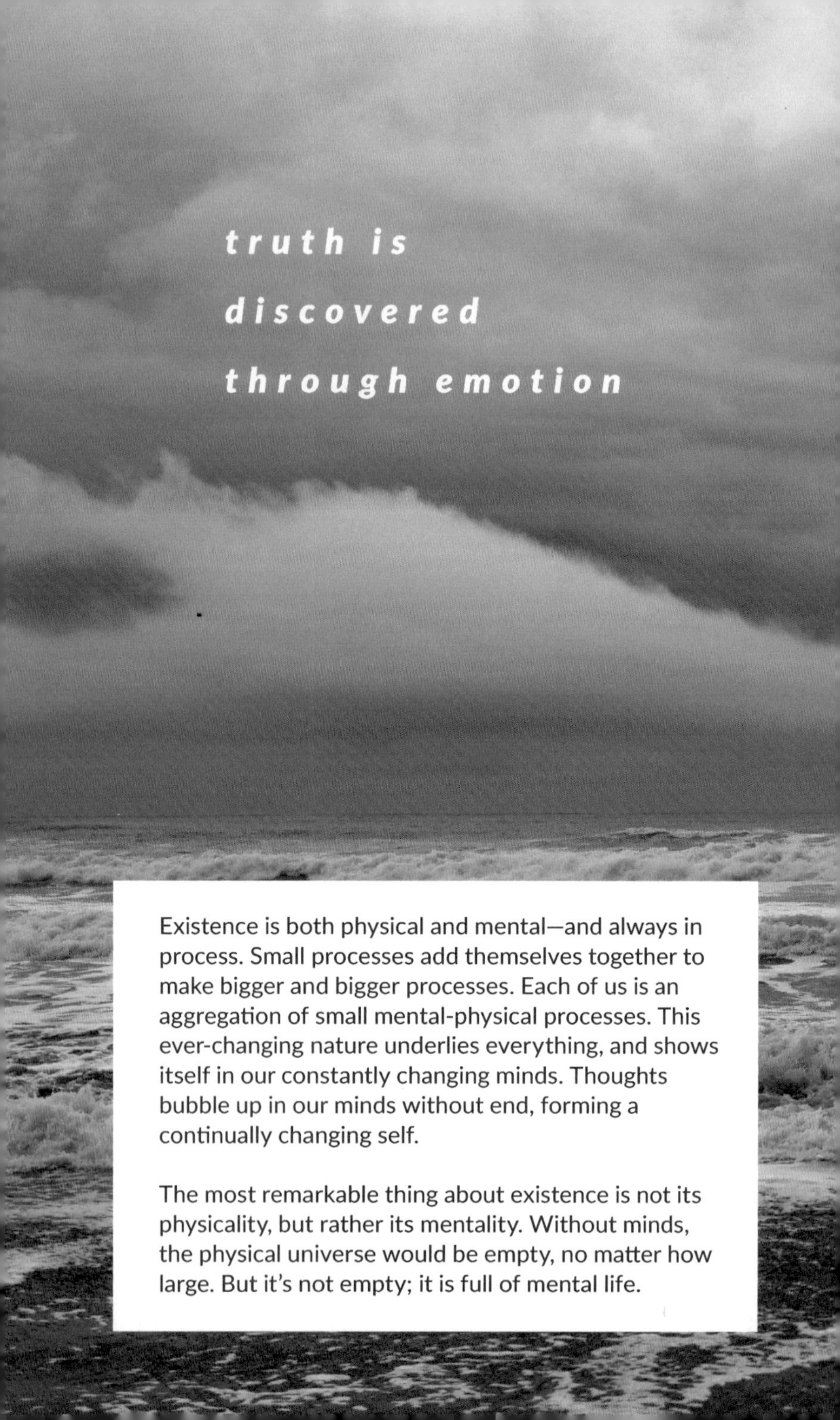

truth is discovered through emotion

Existence is both physical and mental—and always in process. Small processes add themselves together to make bigger and bigger processes. Each of us is an aggregation of small mental-physical processes. This ever-changing nature underlies everything, and shows itself in our constantly changing minds. Thoughts bubble up in our minds without end, forming a continually changing self.

The most remarkable thing about existence is not its physicality, but rather its mentality. Without minds, the physical universe would be empty, no matter how large. But it's not empty; it is full of mental life.

Therefore, above all, we should be concerned about our own minds. We are each born into a particular place and time. We have no control over this. Our genes are forced upon us, for good or ill. Our environment shapes us. Yet, there comes a time when we can begin to order our own thoughts. Through great effort, we can shape our minds regardless of the vagaries of history and chance.

Just as it is in the nature of birds to fly and fish to swim, it is in the nature of humans to think. Through thinking, and controlling our thoughts and feelings, we become more human.

Feeling is fundamental. Many truths are known by reason and we must use reason to learn about the world and ourselves. But all truth is in the end the *feeling* of truth. Reason helps us clarify and illuminate what we know to be true through experience and intuition.

Can color be described by reason? Can you explain the color red to a person blind from birth? No matter how brilliant a scientist you are, color must be experienced. Color is a perception, a feeling. What other truths are like this? Who can explain through reason why anything exists at all? Existence must simply be experienced, it cannot be explained.

If you wish your children, and your wife, and your friends to live forever, you are stupid; for you wish to be in control of things which you cannot, you wish for things that belong to others to be your own. So likewise, if you wish your servant to be without fault, you are a fool; for you wish vice not to be vice, but something else. But, if you wish to have your desires undisappointed, this is in your own control. Exercise, therefore, what is in your control. He is the master of every other person who is able to confer or remove whatever that person wishes either to have or to avoid. Whoever, then, would be free, let him wish nothing, let him decline nothing, which depends on others else he must necessarily be a slave.

- Epictetus

what use is status?

Everyone desires certain things above others. Most people don't even really know why.

Maybe evolution programmed it into them. Maybe they picked it up from the culture they happened to be born into. We believe that fulfilling our desires will bring us happiness. But why should we think that? Where do our desires come from?

Most desires come from the desire for status. People want nice things, not because nice things are nice to have in and of themselves, but because having nice things increases their status. People want flashy cars not because flashy cars have any inherent value, but because of how other people will view them when they're driving around.

Most people want status, simply because they're primates and it's in the nature of social primates to want status. Primates evolved that way. Having high status brings real evolutionary advantages. It gives primates a better selection of mates and better access to food and shelter. We are descended from the apes that successfully fought and killed for high status for millions of years. Their high status enabled them to spread their genes better than their low-status rivals. We have inherited these genes and the desires they encode.

But these desires are not designed to make us happy. They're designed to help us survive. We are survival machines, not happiness machines. Our desires evolved over long periods of time in order to win the struggle for survival and reproduction. Our ancestors wielded the weapon of status in order to eat and mate better than low-status apes. We now indulge in these desires reflexively, without consciously assenting, because we follow our evolved instincts without thought. We simply assume without question that getting the things we want (things that will increase our status) will make us happy. This belief is so deeply ingrained in us it is mostly unconscious.

Yet we all know people who seem to get what they want, and still aren't happy. They chase things, rather than happiness itself. Happiness must be found directly, not through other things.

They're following instincts designed to help them outbreed others. Why should we expect to find happiness there? We believe that if we get some thing, some status, then that will increase our happiness. But this backfires all too easily. Rather than put our hopes and trust in external things, we can work for happiness directly, in our minds. We have little control over external things, and even less control over how other people think. However, we have a lot of control over how we ourselves think.

Because most people allow their happiness to depend on things they don't control, they don't control their own happiness. Their happiness doesn't depend on them and their own actions. It depends on external factors out of their control; it depends on other people's opinions. A better path to happiness, then, is to learn to control your own opinions, your own emotions, your own mind.

Philosophy does not claim to secure for us anything outside of our control. Otherwise it would be taking on matters that do not concern it. For as wood is the material of the carpenter, and marble that of the sculptor, so each individual's own life is the material of the art of living.

– Epictetus

why worry about any of this?

Why bother with any of these ideas at all?

First, thinking is the most human action. It's what's most evolved in humans and gives us meaning. So to be most human we should spend a lot of time thinking

Second, minds are the most important things that exist. The interactions between minds are the things we should value most. To do that, we need to understand as best we can what a mind actually is.

Third, to know how to live we need to understand life and understand ourselves. To do this, we need to study science and philosophy.

If we don't do these things, we live only on the surface of things, like unthinking animals.

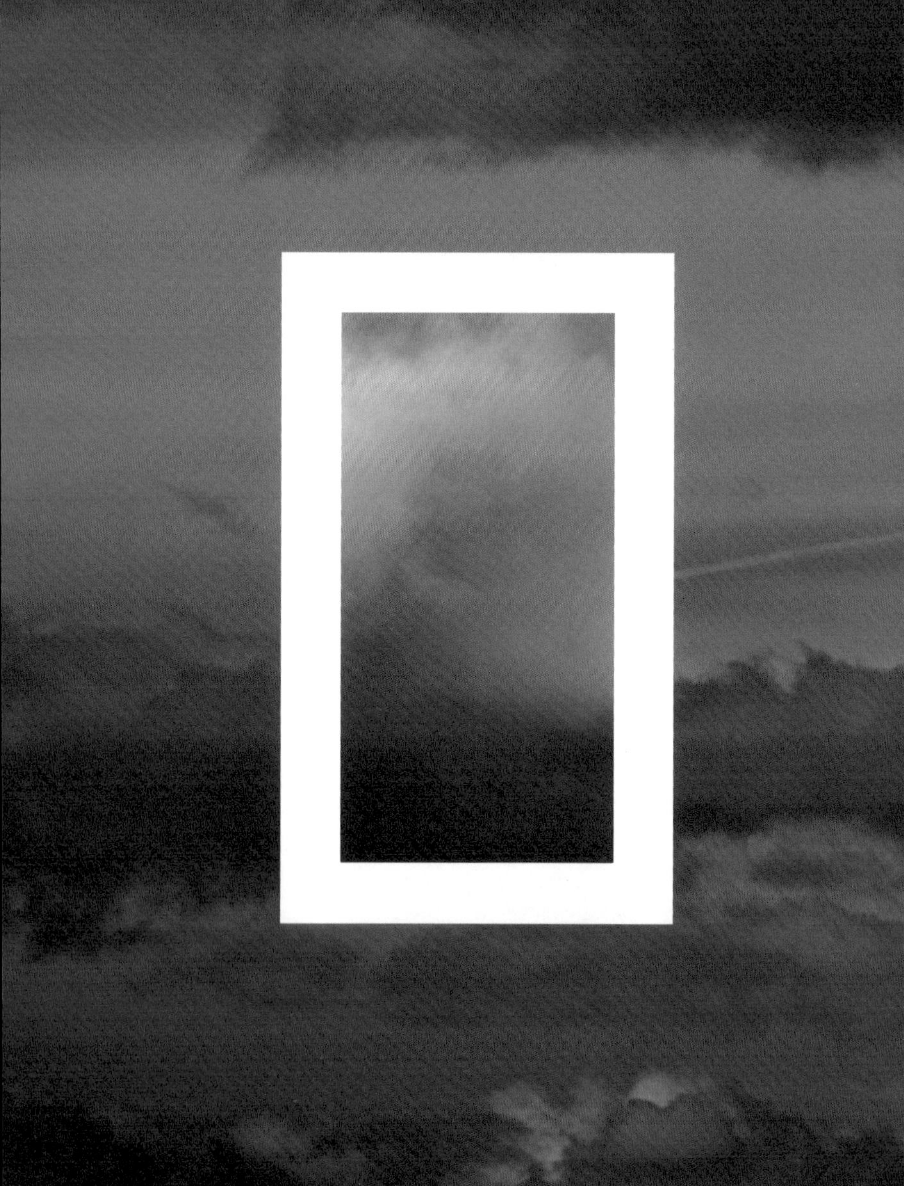

Some things are in our control and others are not. Things in our control are opinion, pursuit, desire, aversion, and, in a word, whatever are our own actions. Things not in our control are body, property, reputation, command, and, in a word, whatever are not our own actions. The things in our control are by nature free, unrestrained, unhindered; but those not in our control are weak, slavish, restrained, belonging to others. Remember, then, that if you suppose that things which are slavish by nature are also free, and that what belongs to others is your own, then you will be hindered. You will lament, you will be disturbed, and you will find fault both with gods and men. But if you suppose that only to be your own which is your own, and what belongs to others such as it really is, then no one will ever compel you or restrain you. You will find fault with no one or accuse no one. You will do nothing against your will. No one will hurt you, you will have no enemies, and you will not be harmed.

– *Epictetus*

happiness & reason

The universe creates life and with it, our emotions; yet the universe does not make all experiences positive. People born into terrible circumstances can experience much suffering and pain, while others benefit from more fortunate circumstances.

Is it even possible to have positive emotions without negative ones? Just look around you, it certainly doesn't look like the universe has happiness as its goal. We might suppose the universe wants happiness but cannot guarantee it. This implies that the universe is embedded in something else—something that sets conditions and limits it. If so, we would have to believe in two things: the universe and something else, some other set of laws.

Perhaps the universe does not want us to be happy. How strange, then, that emotions should exist at all. Why should the universe create beings that can experience pain? Perhaps we just don't understand because we don't see things from the cosmic perspective. We experience life from the viewpoint of a fragile, mortal being. And from this viewpoint, happiness and pain are quite real.

So for a living thing to set happiness as a goal for itself seems presumptuous. If it is not a goal for the universe, how could something lesser think it can achieve what the universe does not want or allow? Yet, we find ourselves unable to stop desiring happiness. This is natural. But the key question is: what kind of happiness is it rational to desire?

We tend to think of happiness as a positive, bubbly emotion—a slightly subdued version of joy. Perhaps we misunderstand the nature and meaning of happiness and confuse it with something else? Happiness worth desiring must be found in rational thought, the tool we most fully control.

Living things have desires and impulses, and because desires are attractive, they pull us toward the object of our desire, unreflectively believing the desire to be inherently good or will lead us toward a good end. We believe that fulfilling desires will increase happiness. Of course, we all know this is not always the case. Many desires exist because in our evolutionary past they enhanced survival, not happiness. Evolution has made us into survival machines, not happiness machines.

Because we happen to be social animals, the desire for social status is innate and deeply ingrained. Many of our desires are really variations of the desire to increase social status. A high-status monkey has survival advantages over other lower-status members of the troupe—for example, access to mates and a greater ability to reproduce. We are the descendants of high-status monkeys who could mate most effectively. This desire for status manifests itself most dangerously as pride, which more often than not leads to self-destructive behavior that ruins our relationships and ends up making us unhappy.

In attempting to increase our own happiness we unreflectively follow our natural desires and instincts. But these did not evolve for our happiness, why then should we expect our happiness to increase when we follow them?

We allow pride and desire for status to dictate our behavior, believing the adoration from others will bring us happiness. Many people will claim that this does, in fact, increase their happiness. But what kind of happiness is that? That is just the base emotion of a monkey dominating other monkeys.

We are faced with a conundrum: Happiness seems like something we want, yet an honest view of the universe reveals it to often be at odds with what the universe wants or allows. Nevertheless, we can't shake the feeling that happiness is good, and we chase it instinctively. But what we believe to be happiness is not in fact worthy of the name. It is a lure generated by instincts that evolved millions of years ago in our ape-like ancestors to increase their ability to survive and reproduce.

True happiness, then, is not a bubbly feeling, but rather a form of understanding. True happiness is understanding what you are and your role in the larger scheme of life. True happiness comes from you giving your own life meaning. It comes from struggle.

True happiness encompasses many positive and negative emotions. True happiness is itself an emotion, yet it is derived through reason. True happiness is a type of peace that comes from understanding and accepting the world as it is.

To experience happiness, we must experience pain. To choose to live well, we must be able to choose to live badly. We are truly free, with all of the beautiful potential and danger that entails. We can experience love because we can experience loss. We feel elation because we feel depression.

Once we understand this, we can let these emotions wash over us without drowning us.

We are simply the universe looking at itself. For the universe to experience happiness, it must experience it through us.

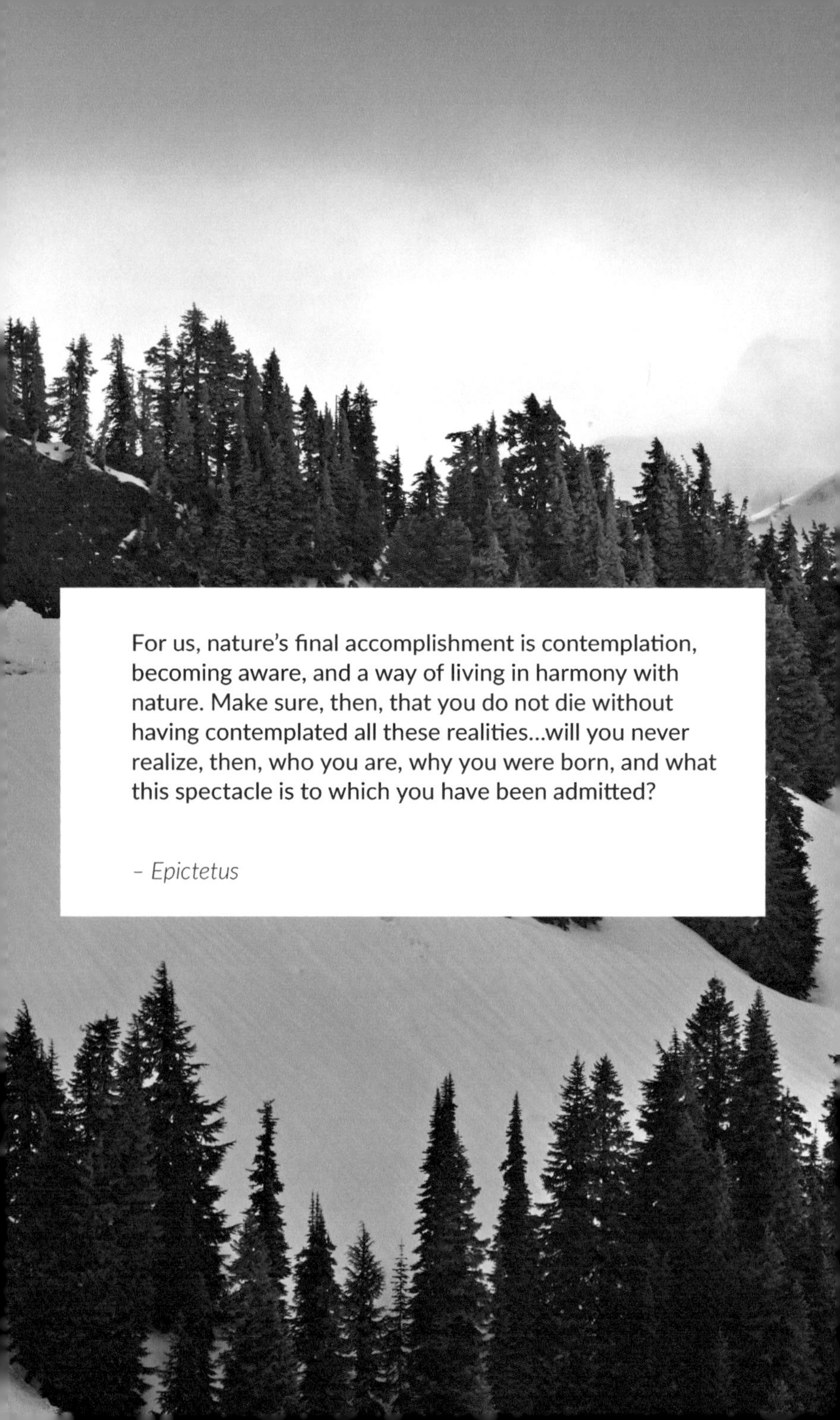

For us, nature's final accomplishment is contemplation, becoming aware, and a way of living in harmony with nature. Make sure, then, that you do not die without having contemplated all these realities...will you never realize, then, who you are, why you were born, and what this spectacle is to which you have been admitted?

– *Epictetus*

the isolation
of the
human mind

Each person appears to him- or herself to be an island of feeling in a vast universe of unfeeling and unthinking matter. We assume other people also to be thinking-feeling creatures, but our inability to feel what they feel *directly* isolates us from others, regardless of how good we are at communicating. Despite our experiential isolation, we are social animals. But because we are unable to feel other people's feelings, emotions, or thoughts we feel trapped inside our own minds. This results in a tendency towards pride and selfishness, made worse by our evolutionary survival instincts honed over millions of years.

We can see the practical effects of these facts everywhere. By nature, people live in their own bubbles. For each of us, reality is confined to what we directly experience. Only with great difficulty can we imagine the lives of other people. Empathy doesn't come easily. The more distant in time, space, and culture other people are, the greater the difficulty of imagining ourselves in their place.

What matters to most people is their immediate surroundings and the vagaries of their social environment. This unavoidably colors everyone's perception of what is important in life. Most people unknowingly decide on their life goals and pursue happiness based on the accident of their birth and the culture they happened to be born into.

The nature of experience further tricks us. Every moment, experience changes. We feel an ongoing series of sensations and emotions, one after the other, like a bubbling stream. Yet we remain convinced of our identities. We feel a strong sense of continuity with our past. In each moment, our minds reach into the past and feel our memories. How could we have this singular point of view if it were not based in a permanent self, a stable observer? Yet where is this observer in the unstoppable stream of experience? Is there really a stable self? Or just a series of momentary experiences?

The self is not a thing. The self is a process, a stream of experiences. All things are like this; nothing is permanent or stable. The self simply changes more rapidly than other things, like mountains, mold, or trees. The difference between life and non-life disappears when we observe things on different time scales.

In each moment, we find only experience, and no self. An ever-changing experience is, in fact, the same as saying there is no self— because if a permanent, static self existed at the base of all of this flux, its unchangeable nature would prevent the changing experiences we actually feel.

Experiences occur everywhere in nature, in some places more concentrated than in others. We are just such a locus of activity, a concentration of experience like the eye of a storm. Although our minds appear to be isolated islands of thought surrounded by unthinking matter, they are more like the crests of waves formed out of a vast sea. Each peak may appear to itself to be separated from the rest of the water, but soon the wave will subside and the peak will dissolve back into the ocean. This apparent isolation is just a temporary happenstance, everything rejoins the single process in the end.

With this realization, we can see the inherent interconnectedness of all things. Nothing is separate, there is only one process. There is not empty space and matter moving through that empty space, that would be believing in two things. There is just the one process, folding in on itself continuously, a turbulent cauldron of creation spewing forth new forms and experiences in a never-ending stream.

What place then can there be for pride once you understand this? Should a beautiful wave fancy itself better than the surrounding ocean which formed it?

what is the

ideal life?

People are born into a particular time and place. From the standpoint of any individual, the circumstances of their birth appear, and might be, random. Why should I be born in this particular place? At this particular time?

Given these circumstances, each person will have a totally unique set of experiences and sensory impressions. Each will see and hear certain things, in a certain time sequence, that no one else will. Because of this, each person has a unique body of knowledge that cannot be adequately conveyed to anyone else in words. In this sense, each person remains totally isolated, no one else can climb inside another person's skin and experience their experiences. We attempt to overcome this through language, art, and shared experiences that we imagine have similar effects on others. Indeed, no one knows for certain that any other person has feelings, because no person can directly experience another's feelings or thoughts. We infer that others have thoughts, feelings and emotions from the fact that other people have bodies and brains similar to ours and behave in similar ways. It simply makes sense, therefore, that other people therefore have feelings, too. We believe this from an early age, and rarely question it. But that is a belief, not knowledge.

We all inherit modes of thought from our particular culture. It is possible to change these mental habits, but it requires much effort, and is rarely done successfully. Typically, these cultural modes of thinking take root at such an early age we hardly ever notice them by the time we become adults. This leads to many difficulties when attempting to answer certain questions. For example, try this: What is the ideal life?

Had I been born into an eleventh-century Mayan culture, what might I have considered an ideal life? How about a North American tribe from 7000 BCE? What if I had been born a German woman in 1902? Are there universal ideals that stretch across the centuries? Is happiness a worthy goal? What is happiness? Is happiness itself universal or does it mean something different to different people at different times? What kind of happiness is worth desiring?

Now picture the times of Vespasian. This is what you'll see: men marrying, raising children, getting sick, dying, going to war, partying, engaging in business, farming, flattering, bragging, suspecting, scheming, hoping for others to die, complaining about hard times, making love or wanting to, making money or wanting to, coveting high office, and seeking to be crowned king. But where is all this teeming life now?

Leap ahead to the times of Trajan, and what will you find? The same, of course, and it too dead and gone. For that matter, examine the history of any people or time. See how hard they strove and how soon they vanished back into the elements from which they were born. But most of all consider those you personally have known who, ignoring the good that lay at their feet, ran after some vain thing and never found the happiness that was within their reach all the time. A man's interest in an object should be no greater than its intrinsic worth. Remember this and you will not become distracted by trivialities or discouraged if you never get around to some of life's details.

- Marcus Aurelius

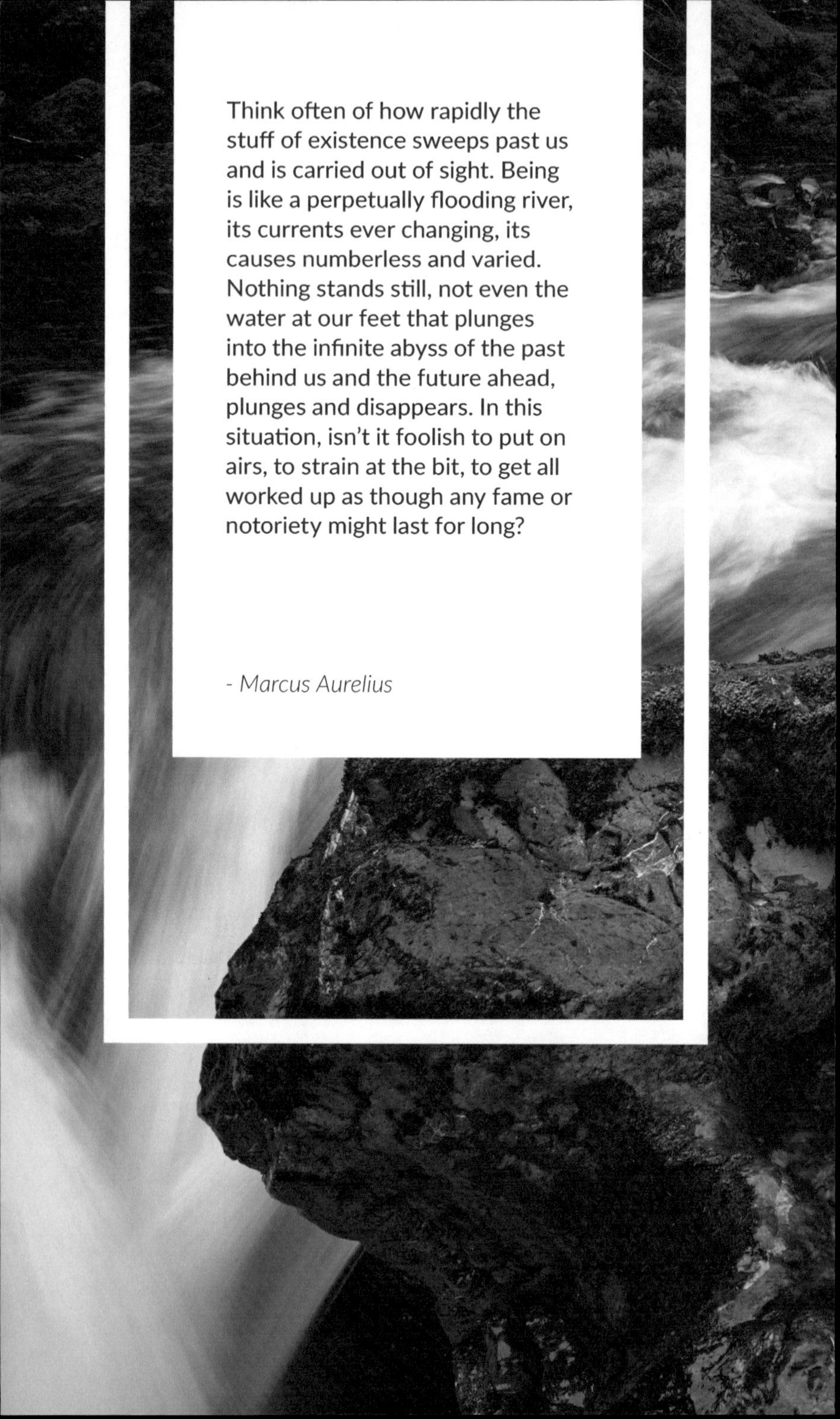

Think often of how rapidly the stuff of existence sweeps past us and is carried out of sight. Being is like a perpetually flooding river, its currents ever changing, its causes numberless and varied. Nothing stands still, not even the water at our feet that plunges into the infinite abyss of the past behind us and the future ahead, plunges and disappears. In this situation, isn't it foolish to put on airs, to strain at the bit, to get all worked up as though any fame or notoriety might last for long?

- Marcus Aurelius

What is life

Existence

Like everyone else, my mind tends to focus on common day-to-day issues: work, family, and problems that need attention. Once in a while, however, I snap out of my everyday thoughts. A curious feeling overtakes me and I'm struck by the strangeness of my existence and everything around me. If philosophy begins with wonder, then the biggest wonder is that anything exists at all.

How strange, for instance, that we stick to the surface of a sphere so big that it appears flat to us. How strange, too, there should be such inaccessible vastness in space. How strange, besides, that this world should be full of so many different creatures, that so many have existed before us, and that so many have already disappeared. What quirks of time and space account for the fact that was I not around back then? Why, I wonder, do I find myself in this particular universe, on this particular planet, at this particular time, in this particular body? Even more mysterious: Why do I have this particular set of experiences I recognize as "mine" and not someone else's? Why should the laws of nature be like this and not something else entirely?

In rare moments of clarity—when I pay especially close attention—everything strikes me as bizarre. All my life I've had a particular, unique, perspective on the world: when I look down I see a chest, waist, and legs. I see my arms and legs. Why don't I ever see the body of a giant moose when I look down? Why don't I ever see myself from above and behind, like in a video game? Why doesn't my perspective move around separately from my body? What creates this astonishing and profoundly mysterious feeling that somewhere between my eyes, somewhere in the middle of my head, I exist? Why can't I project my consciousness somewhere else, and experience things through some other bit of matter? Why is my mind somehow so intimately tied to this changeable and ephemeral body?

Could it be that nothing exists at all? I don't mean empty space or blackness, for that would still be something. I mean truly nothing. No black, no space, no numbers. No empty vacuum, no mathematics. No truth, no laws of nature. In true nothingness, 5 times 5 would not equal 25, for there would be no such thing as "5" or "equals." True nothingness is impossible to imagine. No matter how hard I try, something still pokes in—even if it is only my own awareness or feeling of nothingness. But a feeling of nothingness is not true nothingness because the feeling itself exists.

It still seems logically possible that nothing at all ever existed, yet something does exist. And not only something, but a very particular and unique something—me. Why should I exist at this particular time, in this particular body? I had nothing to do with any of this, yet here I am. I took part in nothing that came before me, yet somehow reality has hurled me forth. Why should it be the case that I have experiences . . . and why this particular sequence of experiences out of the boundless expanse of possible experiences? I've read memoirs of people who lived in the past. I assume they all had inner mental lives something more or less like mine. I've read fragments of writings and letters that have come down to us over the millennia. I've seen cave paintings and archaeological remains of people even before that, before any writing existed. Those ancient folk certainly seem to have experienced things; they, too, had thoughts and emotions. People like me have existed for tens of thousands of years at least—possibly for a couple of million years. They, too, found themselves born into a strange world and experienced a particular series of feelings and emotions created by their actions and by that environment. For instance, someone born in the plains of North America 5,000 years ago: what did he or she believe about the universe? And how strange I should exist now and have no direct experience of them and vice versa. Why were they "they" and I "me"? Why should reality be like this and not some other way?

It's quite simple, you might think. The laws of nature are such that the Big Bang must have occurred and that our universe flows inexorably from that first moment, for reasons that we will someday discover. But why should some law of nature exist that created the Big Bang? Why should any law exist? Have the laws of nature always existed? And what is a law exactly? Is it a mathematical formula floating in some non-physical realm? Before atoms move, do they first check with the laws of nature to see how they should move? Are the laws really there or are they just a type of language that we've created to describe things that we happen to see? Do the laws of nature cause things to behave in a certain way or are they just descriptions of tendencies that we observe in nature? Are they just observations of things we've seen happen over and over, propensities for things to behave in a certain way? Could those laws change tomorrow?

Why should necessity exist? Is there really cause and effect? Couldn't it be the case that sometimes a billiard ball hits another and causes it to move, and sometimes a billiard ball hits another and a pink elephant appears? Why doesn't that ever happen?

Why should even math exist? Is it necessary that 2 + 2 = 4? Could it be the case in some other reality that 2 + 2 = 5? Must 2 added to 2 always add up to 4, or is that just a happenstance of this particular universe? Do we discover math or do we invent it? If nothing physical existed . . . no moon, no stars, no people . . . would math still exist? Or does math depend on something else? Does the world depend on math? Or does the world create math? Why should we be able to describe so much of the world mathematically? Why should that even work? Couldn't it be the case that numbers are just some meaningless abstraction with no relation to physical events—some abstract curiosity that we've stumbled across but with no use in the concrete world? But look at how useful they are! Surely that can't be a coincidence, can it?

Perhaps, you might argue, it's even simpler than that. Everything exists because of God. But, then, why does God exist? People believe he has always existed. But why! Why should anything have ever existed, whether it be for a moment or all eternity, whether it be a natural law or God? We can't keep explaining things in terms of something before it. At some point, something must just simply be. And then, what is that thing that simply is, and why does it have the nature it has? Why that brute fact and not some other? Why is it not some other thing that simply is?

And most bizarrely of all, after all of this bewilderment, not only does something exist, but consciousness exists, too. That truly blows my mind. Let's just accept the brute fact that particles materialize out of seemingly nothing; that a big bang erupted, creating an enormous universe. Fair enough. But why? And then an even deeper mystery: Why does the universe contain minds, sentient beings that feel? Why in the world should I feel anything at all? I always feel something when I'm awake: happy or sad, comfortable or restless, bored or anxious. Colors, smells, random thoughts . . . my mind is always active. A constant stream of consciousness pervades my every waking moment. Perhaps existence would be easier to understand if there were just particles bouncing around with no emotion. . . . but, then, who would be around to understand anything? The universe doesn't just have substantial particles and mechanical laws. It has produced creatures that have emotions, feelings, thoughts—creatures that have experiences and a certain ineffable feeling of being alive.

Many people have attempted to give logical proofs as to why

something must exist, or why God must exist. These all fail. Existence is simply a brute fact. What can I do before the wonder of creation but be astonished?

The Stuff of the Universe

This problem of existence bothers me. I'm sure it bothers a lot of other people, too. But there is a further problem to consider. We who have grown up in the modern era have absorbed its teachings so thoroughly that we don't even notice how they color our views of reality. The modern scientific understanding of things assumes a very particular state of affairs, one that we generally accept without ever realizing it, much less questioning it.

This view is typically called "materialism" or "physicalism." Those aren't terms you hear very often because they form the background of all scientific discourse. Scientists rarely mention them because they are simply assumed to be true. This mechanical view of nature tells us that what "really" exists is nothing but physical reality. Atoms, molecules, electrons, and photons . . . those things are real. Other things, such as emotions, abstract truths, or colors, are somehow assumed to be less real.

According to physicalism, for something to exist it must be measurable in some way. Or rather, by circular reasoning, the things that can be measured are simply the things that "really" exist. For something to be real, it must have a mass, energy or some sort of effect on the physical world. Things that don't have these qualities don't truly exist. This unstated assumption lies behind all of modern science: the physical world is real, and everything else less so—or, worse, doesn't exist at all. The stuff of the universe just is physical—that's the driving assumption behind all modern science.

Physicalism has been remarkably successful in describing the world around us. It has enabled all of the modern scientific progress that has improved our quality of life so much. It helps us explain the structure of atoms, chairs, and mountains. It explains the functioning of so much of what surrounds us. Without a doubt, the mechanical view of nature has produced many discoveries and insights into the workings of nature.

A close corollary to physicalism is reductionism: the idea that all phenomena can be reduced to more fundamental and simpler entities or laws. Although the interactions between atoms and smaller particles may in practice be very complicated, in principle they are relatively simple, and by understanding those interactions we can understand the behavior of much larger and more complicated collections of atoms. According to this view, in principle, with enough cognitive power and enough understanding of the behavior of atoms we could perfectly model the behavior of hurricanes, trees, and mice. Biology reduces to (or is explained by) chemistry, which in turn reduces to physics. According to this view, if you understand physics well enough, you can understand everything.

But physical reductionism has some rather big blind spots. It tells us nothing about the miraculous ability of mathematics to describe the world. Is it just a coincidence that not only does math explain the world, but by exploring mathematical truths we can make predictions about the world that turn out to be physical truths as well? This, in fact, is how much of modern physics advances; many particles have been discovered in this way.

Think about this for a moment: by manipulating symbols according to the abstract rules of math, we can make predictions about physical things. Without this, there would be no such science as particle physics. Modern physics depends, for example, on mathematical symmetry. Physicists might notice a phenomenon in the real world, describe it mathematically, and then notice that the math would be more beautiful if the equation that describes that phenomenon were assumed to have a certain mathematical symmetry. The assumption of symmetry leads to a hypothesis that some other thing must exist in the physical world. It guides scientists as they search for the mathematically predicted thing "out there," and oftentimes when they look, they find it. This principle guided the search for the "god particle," and previously led to the discovery of other particles, such as the positron.

But despite all these astounding successes, physicalism remains completely silent when it comes to mental events such as thoughts or emotions. And, of course, this is its biggest weakness. The fact that consciousness exists is undeniable to each of us. Yet the assumption that matter has no consciousness leads to an intractable problem: how can a thinking thing arise from non-thinking things?

Let's suppose that matter has absolutely no mental qualities whatsoever—that atoms are entirely without thought, feeling, or consciousness. Such bundles of mere matter or energy, obeying physical laws, would have absolutely no capacity for experience. If this is so, then how could a mind arise from a brain? And how could a mind act back upon a brain? What is the relationship between the mind and the body? How could a mind arise in evolution from unmindful things?

If we assume that fundamental particles have absolutely no qualities of mind, then explaining our emotional experiences becomes impossible. If one particle has no mind, what difference does it make how many particles you add together? We are made from many supposedly non-conscious atoms, yet we are conscious. Where do our minds come from then? If each cell has absolutely no mental properties, absolutely no emotions or feelings, then how can adding together 100 billion neurons, no matter how complex their connections, all of a sudden conjure up the joys of watching a sunrise or the taste of apple pie? If one atom has no mind, then presumably ten atoms have no mind, and a thousand or one million atoms would have no mind. But, so the story of physicalism goes, somewhere along the line to 100 billion cells, a mind suddenly appears. How? How could anything come from absolute zero to form even the smallest infinitesimal bit of anything?

Given this view, as we follow along this path from mindless cells to a fully sentient brain, you would be forced to believe that at some point in the history of evolution and in the personal history of each creature the addition of one extra brain cell suddenly initiated the "miraculous" transition from absolutely no mind to the smallest glimmer of mind. Yet this leap from absolutely nothing (zero mind, zero experience) to the minutest trace of experience would involve a leap across the infinite. It would require conjuring something out of nothing. Is this not equivalent to believing in magic? It would be as if adding zero to zero repeatedly results in zero, but all of a sudden adding one more zero could somehow result in 0.000026.

It's important to reflect a little bit on the apparent differences between mind and matter. Matter has mass, we can weigh it on a scale. Can you weigh the feeling of thirst? Or the feeling of being irritated because someone is late and you're waiting in the cold? Yet those feelings are real; when you experience them, clearly they exist. And not only are those feelings real, they affect your behavior. The feeling of irritation makes you call the person you're supposed to meet. The feeling of thirst makes you grab a glass of water. Emotions and other mental events act back upon the physical world.

It is not just that we lack the proper scientific tools at this point in history to pinpoint what happens in the transition from zero to something. Our entire understanding of science would have to change to address this "hard" problem—how brains and minds connect. This problem is "hard" because it involves attempts to explain a difference in kind, not degree. It is a problem of how to go from things that can be measured objectively like mass and weight to things that cannot be measured objectively but only experienced subjectively like thoughts and feelings. Unless the nature of science changes radically, or some groundbreaking discovery is made whereby minds, not mere brain activity, can be directly measured by external tools (don't hold your breath), this problem will remain outside the bounds of science as we currently understand it.

The leap from nothing, from absolutely no mind whatsoever, to even the smallest trace of a mental event would be the most radical break in all of the natural world. Nowhere else do we see breaks like this, everywhere else in nature and in evolution things happen gradually. Life developed slowly, step by step, making even the border between life and non-life difficult to pinpoint. The assumed border between no-mind and mind has no basis in the true nature of things. Minds developed—not from a state of zero mind, but from a state of primitive mentality—slowly, step by step with no hard-edged border between mind and lack of mind—because there is no such thing as something having no mind. There are just different combinations of matter interacting in increasingly complex ways and therefore developing increasingly complex mental abilities.

Two Kinds of 'Stuff'

One way of attempting to deal with this problem is called dualism. It states that two fundamental types of things exist in the universe: matter and mind. Some things are made of matter and some things are made of matter and mind. Chairs are made only of matter, humans are made of matter and mind. The external world, which includes our bodies, is made of matter; our inner world, which includes our thoughts and feelings, is made of mind.

How then does thought arise? In the past, dualists believed in the existence of a soul made of "mental stuff" that was somehow related to the body. This idea is now out of fashion among the scientific community, so the modern way to explain mind is "emergence." According to modern science, mind emerges from the complicated interactions of billions of cells, but does not act back upon those cells. Thought and other mental functions are believed to exist only in healthy, functioning complex brains.

The idea that complicated physical phenomena emerge from the interactions of simpler physical phenomena is not too difficult to believe. But with mind emerging from brain we're talking about something very different. A number of intractable problems immediately arise. How could physical and non-physical things possibly interact? If matter is physical, as we commonly understand it, and thoughts are non-physical, then how could a physical brain create non-physical thoughts? And how could non-physical thoughts possibly act back upon a physical brain? How can two things with absolutely no shared attributes interact? That's the core problem facing dualism.

A different kind of problem, no less intractable, faces scientific materialism: the idea of non-physical thoughts evolving from physical matter. Everywhere in nature, and most especially in evolution, things develop gradually. Complicated life forms develop step by step from simple chemicals. Mind-from-matter emergence does not simply claim that physical brains create more complicated physical things; it claims that physical brains create an entirely new class of thing that lacks any physicality whatsoever—minds!

Think about it: If emergence were true, then at some point in the universe's history, some creature with a brain just slightly too simple to have any emotion would have given birth to a creature with a brain just complex enough to experience the very first emotion. In other words, at some point in evolution, a conscious animal would have been born from a non-conscious mother. This leap from absolutely no emotion, to even the smallest, simplest emotion would represent a radical break with everything that came before it.

This is not like claiming that eyes develop from simple, light-sensitive cells. We can imagine that occurring gradually with relatively little trouble. The question, "which creature first developed the ability to see?" depends on your definition of sight. For example, do plants growing towards the sun qualify as 'seeing'? They are reacting to photons striking their cells, how is that different from you reacting to photons striking the cells of your eyes? But the question, "which creature was first to feel?" does not similarly depend on your definition of feeling. The physicalist's claim of mind emerging from mindless matter is much more radical.

It asserts that pure matter could produce emotions or thoughts, which adds a troubling discontinuity to the natural world.

Anyone who thinks long enough about this complicated and difficult problem should be bothered by it. It is easy to dismiss the issue with words, yet once you feel the true depth of the problem, mere words will not suffice. In the end, either you feel the arguments are good enough or you don't.

To me, both dualism and physicalism are unbelievable. I cannot accept that only physical things exist (physicalism), when all day long I am jolted by emotions and experience my thoughts. And I can't believe that two radically different and separate things exist in the universe, with all of the problems that raises. I can't believe the universe is as complicated as that. At its most fundamental level, it must be simple. The truth is simple, although its realization is multi-faceted and complex.

Therefore, there must be just one kind of stuff in the universe.

One Kind of Stuff

The alternative to dualism is monism: the idea that the universe consists of one kind of stuff—out of which everything is made. Clearly, this primordial stuff has a physical aspect (the world contains objects). Yet we know something else about it, too. The world also contains experiencing subjects with minds. The fundamental stuff must have a mental aspect as well.

Nothing in the universe has a privileged position versus any other thing. The differences are all a matter of degree, not of kind—differences of intensity and complexity, for instance. But, to belong to the one universe, everything must be fundamentally similar to everything else.

It would be strange indeed if my brain were so unique that when I eat something some of the atoms in my food make it to my brain and become conscious, while other atoms become part of my arm—which, according to physicalism, is utterly devoid of anything mental. What could possibly account for this difference?

All atoms, all matter, must be similar; therefore all matter must have some degree of mind or sentience. Whether atoms make it into my brain, to the rest of my body, or form part of a plant or a chair they all must possess some trace of mind or consciousness.

In short, the basic universal "stuff" must have both a physical and a mental aspect. This doesn't mean that everything has the same degree of consciousness as we do, just as not everything has the same amount of mass we do. Things differ in their particular composition, and hence in their particular capacity for thought or emotion. Therefore, it is not true that atoms are absolutely devoid of sentience. As strange as it might seem at first, experience must be there, at the bottom of everything, just as physicality is there too.

Our sophisticated human minds evolved gradually from simpler minds, just as our bodies evolved gradually from simpler forms.

This idea can seem so strange you might find it difficult to wrap your head around it, except through analogy. The concept of fields is uncontroversial in our descriptions of the physical world. The most fundamental theories of physics take for granted the existence of fields of force. We say, for instance, that gravity exists everywhere, yet it does not have the same strength everywhere. Gravity pools and intensifies in places because of deformations or warps in the fabric of space-time. This changes the density of gravitational fields. Like gravity, electromagnetic fields also exist everywhere, but with different strengths from one region of space to another, and individual fields can combine into stronger fields. In reality, separate electromagnetic fields don't exist; they form one universal field with different regions of density and activity. Particles of light are not individual things moving through empty space; instead they are self-renewing excitations of the electromagnetic field. Physically, the field is what truly exists.

Quantum particles behave sometimes as waves distributed in space and sometimes more like particles in one specific place. But a particle is not a hard, spherical thing. It is a flurry of activity, a cloud of energy that changes its density over a certain region of space. The "center" of the particle is merely the average of this denser region of space. Subatomic particles have no sharp edges or boundaries. When two particles collide, it's not like two hard balls coming together; rather what's happening are two fields interpenetrating until the density of each becomes so strong they repel each other.

All of space-time is fundamentally the same. It is one thing deforming itself, folding in on itself, blossoming out, swirling back in, exploding, contracting, and forever changing shape. We interpret these deformations and ripples as the particles out of which everything is built.

In a similar fashion, mind must also be everywhere, although with varying intensities and strengths. As reality folds in on itself, forming ripples and curls, the intensity of mind waxes and wanes like the intensity of electromagnetic or gravitational strength.

When we understand the cosmos this way, the problem of interaction disappears. No interaction is necessary, because there are not two things to interact. From the "inside," matter is experienced as mind; from the "outside," the universal "stuff" shows up as physical extension and activity. However, it's all just the one underlying reality, seen from different perspectives. In evolution, complex minds gradually grew from less-complex minds, just like more complex bodies developed from simpler bodies.

> *Neither is mind material, nor is matter mental; neither is the brain process the cause, nor is it the effect of thought; nor are the two processes independent and parallel. For there are not two processes, and there are not two entities; there is but one process, seen now inwardly as thought, and now outwardly as motion; there is but one entity, seen now inwardly as mind, now outwardly as matter, but in reality an inextricable mixture and unity of both. Mind and body do not act upon each other, because they are not other, they are one.*
>
> *—Spinoza (summarized by William Durant)*

Thoughts and Actions

Maybe you find the preceding arguments unconvincing. What's the problem with the idea that the brain is purely physical and yet creates thoughts?

Another way of approaching this problem is to think about cause and effect. Ask yourself, when you do something, what caused you to do it? Was it a thought or a brain cell?

Imagine you are sitting in a chair and gradually feel thirsty. What is thirst? It is an experience. If you've never felt thirst before, it would be impossible to know exactly what the feeling is; just like it would be impossible to know what red is if you've been blind since birth. Sensations, such as thirst, are real, yet we cannot grab and weigh them. According to the dualistic view, a sensation, an emotion, a thought is non-physical; according to the physicalist view, it doesn't actually exist.

Yet when you feel thirsty, you get up to grab a glass of water. We can easily enough explain the act of getting up through physics, chemistry, and biology. Your brain sends electrochemical signals to nerves throughout your body and coordinates muscle contractions, moving your legs and arms.

But what caused that cascade of activity? Was it the feeling of thirst? But if the feeling itself is non-physical, how could it cause a change in your physical brain? How could a non-physical feeling act upon your brain and cause its cells to fire and coordinate the muscular activity that ultimately results in taking a drink of water? That's the problem of interaction in a nutshell.

Perhaps, you might think, the thought doesn't do anything at all. Brain activity causes the thought and brain activity causes the motion of your legs. The only thing that causes anything is the activity of your brain cells. It simultaneously makes you feel thirsty and solves the problem for you, by making you get up.

But why, then, should reality go to the trouble of creating experiences at all? This utterly bizarre belief tells us that experiences or thoughts have absolutely no effect in the world. If that is true, then the brain activity that causes the feeling of thirst could disappear and there would be no difference in your activity. You would still get up to get a glass of water, but without feeling thirst because the feeling itself isn't what causes you to get up. According to this view, thoughts or emotions don't have any effect in the world. They don't do anything. All mental events could disappear and your brain would keep firing away as normal, moving you about; and no one would be any wiser that you were dead inside.

Clearly this is absurd. To believe that thoughts don't cause actions defies all common sense. In our daily lives, the feeling that our thoughts influence our actions and our actions influence our thoughts is so strong it cannot be ignored. No one lives as if their thoughts and emotions are merely illusions. As I look around, as far as I can tell, everyone lives very much under the control of their thoughts and emotions. I am no different; my body affects my mind as much as my mind affects my body.

I refuse to believe this absurdly strange view that minds are just illusions. And I refuse to deny the feeling I have had continuously throughout my life: that my thoughts influence my actions. Thoughts have an impact. My body influences my thoughts and my thoughts influence my body.

So we're back to the problem of interaction, but now we see it in a way that makes it more immediate and real. The only way out is to see that the interaction isn't there. Thoughts don't exist independently of matter.

It is not the case that matter creates thoughts, or that thoughts affect matter, because there are not two things: thoughts and matter. There is only one thing which seen from the 'outside' appears to us as matter but seen from the 'inside' appears to us as experience. The problem of interaction is false because there is no interaction. Reality consists only of one thing and everything shares in this nature. The nature of reality is simultaneously physical and mental, in all things, always and everywhere.

The Evolutionary Problem

Modern science has a further problem when it comes to the relationship between mind and body. If it is true that only physical things can cause other physical things to happen, then how could minds evolve? If mind and mental activity are non-physical, then how could they possibly give a survival advantage to any creature?

Let's assume that human instincts and emotions evolved under evolutionary pressures for survival. Take fear, for example: it seems reasonable to believe that fear is a useful emotion because an animal capable of feeling fear might be more cautious in certain circumstances, or run away from dangerous situations, and so increase its survival odds. An animal incapable of fear might blindly walk up to a tiger and get eaten.

Many emotions could have similar evolutionary value. Yet how could any of this be true if minds can't cause physical activity? If physicalism is true, then evolution works on our bodies and brains, and the fact that we have also have minds is just an accident, an epiphenomenon. But, then, if this is true, any feelings our ancestors ever had could not have affected their physical behavior. How could fear make them flee a dangerous animal? How could any emotion have given them a survival advantage? We would have to believe that emotions evolved randomly and that we just happen to feel fear in dangerous situations for no related reason. We would have to believe that there is no evolutionary reason at all for the emotions you feel, since those emotions couldn't possibly have affected evolution. This absurd conclusion becomes inevitable if you believe in the separate nature of the physical and non-physical.

What Am I Made Of?

I exist. My mind is real. I know this because I feel my mind directly. It's the only thing I directly experience. In many respects, it *is* me.

My body is also real. However, unlike my mind, I don't know this directly. I don't directly experience my body except through my mind. But I believe my body is real, rationally and intuitively, because to believe that my mind is somehow floating in nothingness, unanchored to my body or anything else seems silly. Thus, the rest of the physical universe is also real and I am embedded in it.

I know through experience, logic, and reason that my existence depends on both physical and nonphysical aspects of reality. I am a thinking, feeling thing—a mental thing. But I am not unique in the universe. Because I am made from the same stuff as everything else, I must be like everything else. Similarly, everything else must be like me. Everything else is a mental thing, too, because mind is an intrinsic aspect of nature. The universe itself is a feeling entity, one I am a part of. Since I am not unique or made from matter different from any other matter, my nature must be universal, hence all things that exist are physical and mental. I am like the universe and the universe is like me.

I know that any description of the universe that leaves out mind is incomplete. It doesn't matter how amazingly accurate physics is in describing the universe; unless it includes the feeling of watching a sunset, it's missing something. Physics, therefore, is necessarily incomplete.

Consider what modern science says about colors. Textbooks describe colors in terms of wavelengths of light. When light of a certain wavelength hits your eye, it causes a cascade of signals through various nerves and into your brain. But is this all color is? If you explained this to someone who has been blind since birth, would they then know what the redness of red is? Color is much more than this. It exists "in here" as well as "out there." If you haven't experienced it, it is impossible to describe or understand. All the knowledge of the physics and chemistry of nerve cells and their interactions is nothing like the knowledge of the direct experience of seeing a color.

I know I'm a thinking, embodied thing, with a physical and mental aspect. But that still doesn't exactly explain what I am. When I think about my nature, I can't find anything constant. My thoughts, feelings, and emotions are in constant flux. Whenever I try to pin them down, they change. What exactly is back there? It's just a stream, a bubbling brook of experiences. This stream of consciousness has been ongoing as long as I can remember. I don't remember a beginning; when I think back to my earliest memories, I just seem to fade in—and, no doubt, someday I'll just fade out.

The cells of my body are not truly "things" in any static sense. They are bundles of activity, processes. My cells have a lifespan shorter than mine; they continuously die, yet somehow I create new cells to replace the old. In this sense, I'm continuously dying and being reborn, recreating myself through metabolism for as long as I can.

The flow of this physical change parallels my mental flow. I experience the latter directly. I am not surprised that my thoughts and feelings flow so much because my body is never still. What is true of me is true throughout the universe. My nature is universal. My stream of experience goes hand-in-hand with the never-ending changes in the physical world around me. Change happens at different speeds: mold grows faster than mountains, yet there is no fundamental difference between the two. They're both aspects of the same flow of nature, one fast and one slow.

I am a vortex of matter, a temporary form created out of the stuff of my surrounding environment. I'm a knot in the fabric of the universe, made of the same stuff as everything else. Does the world flow through me or do I flow through the world? Is there a difference? When I was in my mother's womb, the atoms that would eventually make up my body as a child were spread hundreds of miles away, waiting to make it into the food my mother would eventually eat, and which her body would break down and pass on to me. The process continues today: the atoms of my body ten years from now exist, at this moment, in various places throughout the world, later to be incorporated into the food I will eat and use to rebuild my body in the coming years. Are these atoms mindless? No, but I am not yet thinking through them.

Yet it's not accurate to say the world flows through me, because there's no "me" through which it can flow. There is no "me" separate from everything else. It is more accurate to say that the form of my body and mind is like a wave on the surface of an ocean. The wave is not separate and apart from the ocean, nor does the ocean flow through the wave, for the wave is not a thing through which ocean water passes. Rather, wave and ocean are one thing seen from different perspectives. To an observer, the wave temporarily takes on a form different enough from the ocean to make it stand out from the rest of the ocean. But fundamentally there's just the ocean, taking on many different shapes, constantly surging and undulating.

Process is Fundamental

When I think about the nature of the fundamental stuff of the universe, I tend to think of it as a "thing," like clay. The scientific view has seeped into our culture so much that we now automatically think in terms of "things", such as atoms and molecules. But this isn't precisely accurate. Physical existence at its most fundamental level is a process, not a thing. Quantum physics tells us that the world consists of events, not static objects. Processes form temporary things, but the activity of the process never ceases. Ultimately, everything that exists is part of one universal process, folding and curling in on itself and so creating the appearance of many smaller processes, in the same way an ocean creates the appearance of being made of many smaller waves, eddies, and currents.

The fundamental nature of reality, then, is not any kind of "stuff"; rather it is universal process, ceaseless activity. Everything is made of this endless creativity, and this unstoppable action is reflected in my constantly shifting thoughts. It is reflected in the constant change I see all around, in the never-ending movement of all things. This is why the difference between life and non-life defies detection. Everything is action, everything flows. Everything is full of gods.

Scientifically, we know this is a more accurate description of matter. Atoms are not static things, they are formed from energetic particles, surrounded by clouds of electrons moving at nearly the speed of light. Empty space is not static, even the "vacuum" of space is full of quantum activity, particles forming and destroying themselves continuously. Everything in nature is in a constant state of change. This is not a new view, Heraclitus in the sixth century BCE said "panta rhei"—everything flows. What's new is the mechanical view of nature. To our ancestors, the fact that nature is sentient everywhere was obvious.

Commonsense, Intuition and Absurdity

In thinking about arguments like these, we need something to guide us. I've read a lot of arguments over the years and I've always been more easily impressed by well-reasoned positions than simple claims or dogmatic assertions. Yet no matter how much I try to develop arguments I believe are examples of "pure reason," I have always failed. And I've never found a philosopher who has been able to produce pure reason, either. Even Spinoza, the master of meticulously reasoned arguments, used subtle appeals to emotion and belief.

Even the Enlightenment thinkers we hold up as paradigmatic examples of rationality had an emotional foundation for their arguments. Their view that matter is inert provided an argument for a god that starts the clockwork universe. Their view of matter as inherently insentient created a need for a god who could put a spark of life into fundamentally dead things.

Reason and emotion are intimately intertwined, reflecting the essential unity of mind and matter in the basic fabric of the world. It is impossible to separate the two. Without a doubt, reason has a certain beauty. A well-formed argument is as beautiful as a poem or other work of art. And the experience of beauty, of course, is an emotion. However, we don't appeal to beauty only in philosophy or everyday argument. It is also a cornerstone of science and mathematics. Scientists and philosophers routinely appeal to a theory's simplicity or beauty in arguing why it must be true. The concept of mathematical symmetry, which is really nothing more than an appeal to beauty, is an essential component of discoveries in physics.

I don't think any of this is a coincidence. We have strong intuitions about certain things, because these intuitions reflect features of the world we find ourselves in and we are very good, in general, at understanding our world. Over time, these intuitions form into a type of commonsense that we ignore at our own peril. Not all commonsense is correct, of course, and I think it's important to distinguish between "elemental" and "secondary" commonsense. Elemental commonsense are the ideas that we all assume in our daily lives that are impossible to deny, because we at least implicitly behave as if they are true—for example, that we are conscious, that we make free choices, and that the past and future are real. Even if we could construct clever logical arguments purporting to show that one of these is false, we all behave in our daily lives assuming they are, in fact, true. Secondary commonsense notions, by contrast, are culturally generated ideas that might seem second nature to us, but are not based on such a deep, undeniable intuition as elemental commonsense—for example, that time flows at a constant rate, that the world is flat, and that the moon changes its shape.

Science and reason can lead us to startling discoveries or new ways of thought. They can just as easily lead us to absurd beliefs. Many people would no doubt argue that the beliefs I promote here are absurd. I have certainly been guilty of following a belief to its logical conclusion only to suddenly realize that I would be forced to believe something I found absurd, something that contradicted elemental commonsense.

Science and reason have been incredibly successful at overturning commonsense beliefs that our most of our ancestors probably held since the dawn of our species. But not all commonsense can be so easily overturned by logical arguments. Elemental commonsense is part of the foundational fabric of our worldview, something so basic that even if someone claims to deny it, they cannot be taken at their word.

Absurdity

Commonsense, based on visual perception alone, tells us the world is flat, science tells us it is round—something we can verify for ourselves by flying high enough or by viewing photos of Earth from space. Commonsense tells us the sun and moon are the same size; science shows this is wrong. With the benefit of hindsight, we can see why, in many cases, the commonsense view feels so strong, and why it is wrong. But some commonsense notions cannot be so easily rejected, no matter how seemingly clever the argument. These are the elemental commonsense notions. When I first came across the argument that consciousness doesn't exist,

I couldn't believe it. How could someone make a claim that every second of their waking lives dispels? How can you deny that your feelings exist? How, in fact, can you doubt or deny anything if you don't possess consciousness? After all, only a creature with consciousness could ever doubt or deny anything at all.

Or how about the claim that although consciousness does exist, it doesn't "do" anything? When I first came across this view, I admit it was seductive. Sometimes the bolder an argument is and the more it runs counter to our commonsense, the more dazzling it can appear. So many of the theories of physics are like this, and we have grown used to having to accept them after the evidence piles up, regardless of how strange or counterintuitive they first seem. Time isn't constant and changes depending on your speed or the presence of massive objects close to you. Space and time aren't separate things, but one thing. Quantum particles don't behave in entirely predictable ways, but only according to certain probabilities. And on, and on, and on.

But the idea that our minds don't actually do anything, that they are like a vapor emanating from our brains, dissipating into nothing, with no effect on our bodies, is just too absurd to believe. It took me a little while for the absurdity of this idea to sink in. One day, I realized that if this absurd notion were true, then all thought and emotion could disappear from the universe and everyone would keep behaving exactly the same as they did before! For if our minds don't do anything, then whatever you think and feel is meaningless—indeed, not only meaningless, but also utterly impotent and ineffective. And, of course, this flies in the face of our daily experience. According to the mainstream scientific view, your brain cells will fire exactly the same regardless of what you think or feel. If your thoughts and feelings were to somehow disappear, your brain cells would keep firing away just as before. The thoughts you've had in the past would have had no impact on the thoughts you have now and the thoughts you will have next. The absurdity of such a claim should be self-evident with a little reflection.

Although this view is nonsensical, it's very easy to reach. It follows naturally from a cursory review of the current, mainstream scientific paradigm. If only physical things are truly real, and molecules have no mental properties, then minds can't affect physical molecules and, therefore, the thoughts you're having now won't affect the thoughts you'll have in the future. Only your physical brain state matters, only that can determine the next physical brain state you will enter. And since according to this view physical means "non-mental," your inner mental life doesn't matter at all. It cannot affect what you will think one second or one year from now. Absurd but logical . . . if you accept the premise that matter is non-mental.

Elemental Commonsense Notions

It's difficult to construct a purely rational argument against beliefs like these. But it's also difficult, and actually impossible, to construct purely rational arguments for other ideas that we all believe and presuppose in our day-to-day activities. For example, can you prove that other people are conscious? Even if you took a brain scan, measured the activity of someone else's brain cells or did some other sort of physical measurement, what exactly would you be proving? Only that physical activity occurred. To prove that they are conscious, you would have to somehow get "inside" their minds and feel their consciousness directly. Naturally, this is impossible, but it's no reason to deny that everyone else is conscious. I can reflect on the peculiarly subjective nature of my mind, without resorting to the belief that only my mind exists since it's the only one I feel directly. That other minds exist is an elemental commonsense notion.

And similarly, there are other elemental commonsense notions that I cannot reject, no matter how amazing the argument against them. These irrefutable commonsense notions form the invisible background of my daily life. For example:

That the external world is real. It could all be a figment of my imagination, but it would be absurd for me to believe that the only thing that exists is my disembodied mind, somehow floating in nothingness and creating the illusion of a physical world around me.

That there is such a thing as cause and effect, and the things I see happening around me aren't just due to coincidence. If a billiard ball hits another ball, and the second ball moves, it's because the first caused the second to move.

That the past and future are real. My mind is not creating the illusion of the past, even though I can no longer feel the past except through the memories of my mind right now. Likewise, there will be a future, even though I never experience it, just the omnipresent now.

That my emotions are real.

That my body influences my mind, and my mind influences my body.

That my mind is unified, even though I know it's somehow derived from many different physical (and mental) things.

That I'm free and I make choices between genuine alternatives. When I do something, it's the case that I could've done otherwise. My actions have not been pre-determined by the laws of physics.

That my mind somehow interacts with abstract notions, like mathematical truths, even though the nature of those things is very mysterious.

What Do We Truly Know of Nature?

I alternate between confidence in my ability to understand the world and despair that it's all too enigmatic. The feeling of despair sometimes turns into wonder at the mystery of it all. Wonder brings with is a very special feeling all its own, a bittersweet combination of hope and surrender.

There's no denying the remarkable advances that science and technology have made and what this has meant for our physical well-being. Scientific progress has been based on a certain view of nature that sees everything as mechanical and suitable for study and understanding by reducing everything to its smallest parts. Yet its very success has created a new orthodoxy that can cloud our judgment. It has removed the spiritual from nature, despite the obvious presence of something sacred all around us. I've witnessed this in myself over the years, as my awe at the explanatory power of mechanistic and impersonal science led me to a pure physicalist, atheistic view of reality. Not until I crashed headlong into the mind-body problem did the sheer implausibility of that view sink in.

The effectiveness of mathematics in describing the natural world has always seemed particularly mysterious to me. Why should math work at all in telling us about physical stuff? About the mud that drips between my fingers or the rays of sun that warms my skin? And how can it be that independent mathematical discoveries made centuries apart have turned out to be intimately linked?

For example, although the numbers e, i, and π were discovered independently in totally different branches of mathematics, the equation $e^{i\pi}+1 = 0$ is true. How? Why? Does mathematics arise from some deep structure within reality itself, or do we project mathematical ideas onto reality? Is mathematics a human invention, and if not—then what exactly is it?

But perhaps these aren't the right questions to ask at all, perhaps a better question is: what do we truly know of nature?

> *Physics is mathematical not because we know so much about the physical world but because we know so little: it is only its mathematical properties that we can discover. For the rest our knowledge is negative. . . . The physical world is only known as regards certain abstract features of its space-time structure—features which, because of their abstractness, do not suffice to show whether the physical world is, or is not, different in intrinsic character from the world of the mind.*
>
> *—Bertrand Russell*

Science tries to be entirely impersonal and objective, yet the world as we experience it is entirely subjective. The only way we learn about the objective world is through entirely subjective experiences. Each of us is isolated in our own consciousness with only imperfect means of communication available. The knowledge each of us possesses is entirely private and unique. What each of us knows, no one else can possibly know—at least, not the way each unique individual knows it. We communicate because we assume that others must have inner experiences similar to ours. If we didn't assume this, what would be the point of even trying to communicate what we feel and know? But the knowledge each of us possesses by virtue of our unique experiences is incapable of being truly known by anyone but ourselves.

Even if I attempted to describe to you the feeling of swimming in the ocean—the feeling of the cool water and my body's slippery movements as I glide through it—that feeling wouldn't exist as a single feeling, distinct from everything else I feel. When I swim in the ocean, all of the other experiences of my life up to that point form a rich tapestry of thoughts and emotions that provide the basis for the sensation of the water at that particular moment. As I swim through the ocean, many other emotions, thoughts, and experiences flow through my mind because of my unique personal history. It is impossible to separate just the feeling of swimming in the ocean from the other mix of emotions and thoughts I have. In order for you to truly understand my particular feeling of being in the ocean, you would have had to live my entire life up to that point. Everything we know is necessarily and thoroughly subjective. So how can anything be truly objective, as science claims?

Modern physics assumes that everything in the universe is physical and that the definition of physical excludes mental events and experiences of any kind. Yet the only way we learn about the external world is precisely through our personal experiences. So if physics is true, then how can we know it is true? Because physics is based on the fundamental assumption that only physical objects are real, wouldn't the very truth of physics mean that our experiences, which are non-physical, are somehow unreal? Yet our knowledge of physics (as of everything else) comes only through those very same experiences. So if they are unreal how could we use those experiences to know that physics is true? It is logically inconsistent to claim that the truth of something denies the only way you having of learning that truth, yet still claim that truth on the basis of that very thing which you deny.

I think it is undeniable that our current physics is incomplete, just taking a bite of chocolate cake is proof enough. Imagine that a scientist was able to scan all of the physical activity of your body for ten seconds while you eat chocolate or watch a sunset. Imagine that scientist had the most advanced knowledge of physics, chemistry, and the laws of nature. Imagine he could describe the activity of every single cell in your body, every atom and every fundamental particle in those atoms. He could write a document trillions of pages long with the most detailed physical descriptions of the activity of your cells. But if that description does not include the feeling of watching that sunset, the experience of colors exploding in your mind and the warmth of the last rays of sun hitting your face, wouldn't that description be incomplete? And even if he did include a description, what words could he possibly use to convey the actual experience of watching the sunset? Any verbal or written description of that experience can merely point the way, but it is a hollow substitute for the real thing.

If this hypothetical physical description of a mere ten seconds is incomplete, how can any description of the universe that doesn't include emotions be complete? A complete description of what happens in any ten seconds of the universe would have to include my experiences and yours and every other living person's. These experiential descriptions would have to reach farther and farther back into the previous emotional lives of each person and animal, in order to truly capture the feeling of those ten seconds. Where could this description stop? In order to be legitimately complete, it would have to describe everything, for all time. It would have to be a perfect description of reality. But it would have to be more than that—it would have to be the actual experience of reality.

And so, our current scientific descriptions of reality are woefully incomplete. How can I believe them, when I know the difference between the chemical structure of sugar and the experience of sweetness? How can I believe that color is merely a wavelength of light, when I can feel the richness of the sight of a forest undulating in a storm or experience the burst of light of sunrise behind a mountain? There is much more than wavelengths of light and electrochemical signaling between brain cells happening there.

And how can I truly know anything about the world around me, when the difference between what is presumed to be merely physical and what happens in my mind is so vast? Am I to believe that joy is a mere pattern of brain cells firing? That is not what joy is, although it may be related to, or somehow dependent on, that. The true nature of the real is wonderfully mysterious. It includes stones rolling down hills. Grass waving in the wind. Stars forming in massive galactic clouds floating in space. The delight of a burst of flavor from a tasty slice of cake and the pleasure of lazy afternoon nap. Mathematical truths and minds erupting with conscious experience. The idea that all of this is reducible to physical events utterly devoid of mental properties is ludicrous.

> *The recognition that our knowledge of the nature of the objects treated in physics consists solely of readings of pointers [on instrument dials] and other indicators transforms our view of the status of physical knowledge in a fundamental way. . . . How can this collection of ordinary knowledge be a thinking machine? But what knowledge have we of the nature of atoms that renders it at all incongruous that they should constitute a thinking object? . . . .Science has nothing to say as to the intrinsic nature of the atom. . . .*
>
> *The atom is, like everything else in physics, a schedule of pointer readings [on instruments dials]. The schedule is, we agree,*

attached to some unknown background. Why not then attach it to something of a spiritual [i.e., mental] nature of which a prominent characteristic is thought. It seems rather silly to attach it to something of a so-called concrete nature inconsistent with thought, and then to wonder where that thought comes from.

We have dismissed all preconception as to the background of our pointer readings, and for the most part can discover nothing as to its nature. But in one case—namely, for the pointer readings of my own brain—I have an insight which is not limited to the evidence of the pointer readings. That insight shows that they are attached to a background of consciousness.

—Sir Arthur Eddington

Truth is Discovered Through Emotion

Feeling and matter are fundamental. Reason must be used to its limits, but beyond those limits lie feelings, sensations, emotions and intuitions. The boundaries of knowledge accessible to us through reason are constantly expanding, yet even reason itself is sculpted from raw feelings and emotions. When we hear a convincing argument, how are we convinced of its truth? Isn't our knowledge of truth itself a feeling or intuition, regardless of how supposedly logical the argument is?

Because mind is an integral property of everything, and our only way of knowing anything is through feeling, the fundamental truth must ultimately be known by feeling. All "truth" is, fundamentally, aesthetic (feeling) and emotional. Formulations of the truth in reasoned arguments can help point the way, but the truth itself cannot be fully known or expressed in words, equations, or arguments. The truth about the nature of reality is a feeling, one that periodically erupts in short bursts when we contemplate deeply enough. With practice, we can feel truth for longer and longer periods; but, in the end, the fullness of truth remains elusive, and disappears as soon as our minds return to more mundane things.

Ultimately, everything I say about reality is false and incomplete. I can say nothing true. Reality must simply be experienced. I'm reduced to using analogies to provide clues. All I can do is point vaguely in its general direction and hope that you see what I'm seeing and saying. If I were a painter, I would try to express this visually, but that would be just as false as using language. If I say that reality is physical, that is false. And if I say that reality is mental, that, too, is false. Even if I say reality is mental and physical, that is also false. Reality is not big or small, finite or infinite. It is not short or long, in time or outside it. Reality doesn't care about me, nor does it ignore me. It does not speak, nor is it silent. It is not light or dark or good or bad. It doesn't live, nor is it dead. I have no knowledge of it yet I know it's there. It is everywhere but I can never see it. I am nothing but *it*, yet I have no idea what I am.

Lack of a Permanent Self

When I look back upon my life, I can't find a beginning. My memories slowly fade in, hazily in fits and starts. At what point did I begin to exist? Was there a single moment where it can be said I existed, right after a moment when I didn't exist? Nature doesn't seem to work like this, and in my life I find no hard edges, no moments where things change unequivocally from this to that, from asleep to awake, from life to death. When I fall asleep, I fade out and I notice the fading only if something startles me awake.

I've learned that only mammals give birth to mammals. If I take this back through history, then every mammal had a mammal as a mother. Yet we know that reptiles evolved before mammals. Does that mean that, at some point, a reptile gave birth to a mammal? Of course not, the evolution of mammals was gradual. There are no hard edges in nature. Mammal and reptile are arbitrary categories we have created to help us understand nature—but those categories don't really exist, except in our minds.

Similarly, at some point I was in my mother's womb, gradually developing. While I was no more than a tiny bundle of cells in the womb, the atoms and molecules that would eventually make up my body as a child existed far away, widely dispersed in animals and vegetables yet to be eaten by my mother. Later on, her metabolism broke down the food and she passed on some of those molecules and atoms to me. Unknowingly and unconsciously, I assembled myself from those bits of matter that had recently been scattered in the environment around my mother and me. Some of that matter assembled itself into my feet, some into my hands, and some into my brain. Was there any difference between the matter that made its way into my hands and the matter that made it into my brain?

This process continues, of course. I am not a "thing," a static object. Rather, I form a slowly changing pattern of activity in time. As water flows through a river, the water molecules change from instant to instant. The river itself is never made of the same molecules of water from one moment to the next, yet the river exists all the same. In a similar way, matter constantly flows through me. Or, to be more precise, the flow is me. I am a flow of biological matter just as a river is a flow of water. My body constantly decays, but, as I eat, my metabolism breaks down the matter I ingest and I use it to constantly rebuild myself. The process of literally incorporating matter that began in my mother's womb continues every moment of my life since then.

My body is made up of ten trillion of my own cells and another 100 trillion bacterial cells. But my cells are in a constant state of decay and repair. Every day, ten billion cells die and are replaced. The average age of a cell in my body is seven to ten years, and many live much briefer lives than that. The cells lining my stomach last only five days. Red blood cells travel a thousand miles through my circulatory system in a short 120 days, before being destroyed in the spleen. The cells that make up the surface layer of my skin are replaced every two weeks. My liver is completely replaced every 300 to 500 days. Even bones, which seem so tough and permanent, are in a constant state of decay and repair. My entire skeleton is replaced every 10 years or so.

Am I the cells that make up my body today? What about the cells that made up my body ten years ago? Who was that? What connects "me" (my current flux of cells) to the matter that once was me but no longer is?

Perhaps my "self" is in my mind, but when I look for it there I don't find it. Moment by moment, new experiences happen and then they're gone. There's nothing permanent in my mind, just a never-ending series of perceptions. Who is perceiving those? No one is—there's nothing other than the flow experiencing itself. There is no person watching those experiences go by, like a man in a movie theater. There is just the stream.

A little bit of praise, and my ego inflates. But what is there to inflate? An insult, and I am hurt. But what is there to hurt? My fleeting mind perceives itself in this world and it wants to find permanence where there is none.

My mind is real and, in each moment, is unified. At every moment, I experience one single perspective on the universe, but there is no single thing that is me.

We like to believe that some things have single causes. When our ancestors saw the sun, they imagined a chariot pulling it across the sky. But no one thing causes the sun to move like that, just the gravitational pull of trillions and trillions of atoms in the sun turning our planet. Likewise, there's no one thing that is me.

My mind exists as the coalescing of the mental aspect of the countless billions of fundamental processes that form my body. For now, those processes unify into my experience. At some point, they will disperse and my metabolism will be unable to repair itself. Will those particles stop experiencing—or will it be just me, a self-identifying ego, that comes to an end?

The Super-Organism

My experience is remarkably unified. Every moment I experience something, it feels like there's a single me. I know a lot more goes on in the background of my mind, yet it is not always accessible to me. When I drive, I sometimes suddenly find myself at my destination, unaware of making every turn or stopping at every traffic light. I must have stopped at all of the lights, but my awareness was focused elsewhere.

Yet despite many, often-disjointed, things going on in the recesses of my mind, my experience is unified, albeit always changing. How can my mind—a single mental unit— arise from so many particles, separate mental units? If the basic particles out of which everything is made each have a mental aspect, how do they unite into a single momentary consciousness? When it comes to the mind, it seems analogies with physical phenomena are hopeless. But I can see no other way to attempt an explanation.

In nature, subatomic particles create small fields that combine into larger fields. Particles have electrical charges, each of which forms a small electrical field. The charges, in fact, are nothing more than regions of different densities in the underlying electromagnetic fields. These small fields combine into larger electromagnetic fields. The mental units of the fundamental stuff must behave in a similar way, like tiny drops of water merging together to form a single pool. .

Or consider ants. Each one behaves in a simple way, yet together they form a super-organism: a colony. The colony behaves in much more complicated ways than any single ant, yet it's nothing more than thousands of ants put together. The colony influences the behavior of individual ants while at the same time each ant influences the behavior of the entire colony. The behavior of neither individual nor group can be analyzed independently of the other.

The super-organism emerges from many individual organisms, just as I do. I emerge from many individual cells, cells that in our distant evolutionary past were once free-living, individual, single-celled organisms. This type of emergence occurs everywhere in nature. A single water molecule is not liquid, yet many water molecules combine together to form a liquid. But when each molecule of water combines with others, does it undergo a fundamental change? Does it become something different than it was? Analysis reveals that nothing fundamental changes in the molecules—although new behaviors and qualities emerge when many water molecules combine—turning gases of individual molecules into a unified liquid.

My mind is the same. It emerges from many individual, relatively simple neurons. In some way, each neuron possesses a small mind. Yet, somehow, together they create my unified mind.

Other People's Thoughts

I feel my own thoughts directly. No one can deny his or her own experiences; but what about the experiences of others? How do I know that my friends have emotions?

If a friend cries, you assume she's sad. And if she laughs, you assume she's happy. But you don't really know she's sad, you just assume it based on her words and other behaviors. Unless you can somehow get inside her head and directly experience her emotions, you can't know for sure.

Perhaps some sort of brain scan could solve the debate, you might argue. But what would a brain scan prove? Even if it were so advanced as to let you watch the movement of individual atoms, what would that show you? You might see a lot of physical activity, but where is the emotion? At best, you might scan your own brain and take note of the feeling you experience as you observe the physical activity that shows up in the scan. Then, by scanning someone else's brain and seeing similar activity, you might conclude they must be feeling something similar to what you felt. This very reasonable assumption is almost certainly true (at least partially), but it's a belief, not knowledge. You can't know with absolute surety that the emotion is really there unless you could somehow get "inside" the other's head and feel it yourself. And even if you did, whatever you might feel would automatically and instantly become your feeling.

Or imagine a different universe, exactly like this one, with the same natural laws, where everything works the same as it does here—except no one feels anything. But that wouldn't matter! In this alternative universe, people still get married, they just never feel love. They make art, they just don't feel beauty. Their brains function exactly like ours, and therefore they behave just as we do. All physical attributes of the atoms, including how they move and interact in the brains, would be the same and, therefore, their behaviors would be the same.

In this "zombie" universe, no-one could ever sense the redness of red or the warmth of heat, or ever experience being alive. In "Zombie World," all that exists would be nothing more than physical things banging around. In that hypothetical universe, animals just as complicated as us, could evolve (without, of course, any inner drives, such as fear or curiosity).

In our world, when we see a dangerous animal, electrochemical spurts of activity change our brains and activate our muscles to flee danger—and we feel fear. In the alternative universe, exactly the same physical events and changes would happen; the same chemical changes would occur, muscles would contract, and animals would flee—all without the slightest trace of fear, or any other experience.

Clearly this is absurd. Without feelings and emotions, our behavior would be impossible. There can be no love and no art without feeling. We flee dangerous animals because we feel fear, which causes the muscles in our legs to contract. Our minds are not mere passengers in our bodies, along for the ride. Our experiences do not dissipate from our brains into nothing, like smoke wafting from a chimney. We cannot accurately describe the world without its emotional content. Physical activity in the brain does not depend only on other physical activity. Physical and mental aspects are so deeply intertwined in the fundamental stuff of the universe that one cannot be said to exist without the other.

Mind-Imbued Stuff

And so I must conclude that the stuff of the universe possesses mind. To be more precise, the matter of our world is not merely physical "stuff." It is also non-physical; and it is not stuff at all—it consists of psycho-physical events and processes. Life is not a mere accident of random collisions of "dead" matter, and mind is not just a side-effect of physical evolution. Experience is not an accidental curiosity occurring on a small planet aimlessly orbiting one of the numberless stars. Mind, I conclude, is central to the nature of physical reality. Mind and experience exist as aspects of everything, part of the fundamental fabric of the universe. Experience, then, is as fundamental to matter as mass.

Do Things Exist for an 'Instant'?

Reality is not made of "things." What we conceive of as atoms are ultimately composed of energy constantly in flux. The ultimate stuff of reality, then, is not things or "stuff," but process.

Time and change are fundamental aspects of everything. Because of this, nothing can exist in an instant. Everything exists as part of a process—always in transition and undergoing transformation. Even the tiniest process (e.g., a quantum event) requires a minimum duration of time. Nothing exists apart from other things or apart from time.

When I take a breath, at what point do the molecules of air I've inhaled become part of my body? Whenever I exhale, am I disposing a part of me into the environment?

My brain requires a minimum amount of time to fire its neurons. My thoughts require a minimum amount of time to be coherent. Experience is never instantaneous; it exists only in time. A process apart from time is nonsensical. The universal process is time itself. Experience constantly changes, because matter is constantly changing. The unstoppable process of reality involves perpetual transformation, renewal, and regeneration. Because of this, we can never pinpoint a permanent self.

If I wasn't continuously transforming, I would have no experience. If I were unchangeable, I would experience nothing, because to experience something requires change. To experience simply *is* to change. Each moment must be different. If all of the moments of my life were the same, what would I experience?

Likewise, the universe constantly changes, constantly experiencing new things. I am just a reflection of the reality of nature. That reality is change.

Does the Universe Have a Mind?

When we think of empty space, we imagine objects moving through it. We imagine something empty with substantial things moving through it. But this cannot be the case because it would mean that fundamentally two kinds of things exist—space itself and its physical contents. In reality, all that exists is one universal process. What we perceive as individual things moving through empty space are really just knots in the fabric of space-time rippling through the universal process. Everything is part of one interconnected process; there are no separate, individual particles moving through a void, only dynamic wrinkles in the fabric of reality. Everything is made of this. As we know from our own experience, this "fabric," this universal process, is both physical and mental.

Therefore, it stands to reason that the universe as a whole could very well be conscious. Since all matter has a mental aspect, the complicated structure of the universe itself could generate a consciousness.

What kind of feelings or thoughts does the universe have? We will never know. Perhaps that is the source of mathematics and why abstract notions such as justice and reason are so important to us. Does the universe want things like we want things? Or is desire an artifact of our particular size, our contingent historical evolutionary past and our peculiar brains? Does reality have goals? If we have goals, and we are part of nature, why would it be so ridiculous to think that nature itself has goals as well?

But most importantly, why should the universe create us?

If the universe is alive in some way, if it has thoughts in some way, we are we here? Why does it need us?

To think that the mind of the universe could in any way be compared to our own minds is an enormous error. Whatever the universe is doing, it is something that completely transcends the way we think, feel and act.

Yet the very fact that we are here is in indication that what we do is not meaningless.

The answer I think lies in the bittersweet experience of existing. In order to experience happiness, you must know what sadness is. In order to experience joy, you must know what pain is.

This is true, even for the cosmos itself.

What we are, is the universe looking at itself, experiencing itself. For reality to feel happiness, it must feel it through us because happiness requires a mortal existence. Happiness requires a life that knows it can experience true loss and death.

It is the finite nature of our existence that gives each moment infinite value. In order to experience that, the universe must form itself into temporary, finite beings. In order to feel happiness, the universe must form itself into small beings that sometimes are sad. In order for the universe to experience morality, it must create the freedom to do immoral things.

And so our lives are not meaningless or cosmic accidents. We are the cosmos itself, living through itself to experience beautiful moments that can only be experienced by frail, flawed, mortal beings.

How to Live

First I must decide what life *is*, then I can decide *how* to live.

I must have a theory of what nature is, what reality is, why I am here at this place and this time. My beliefs about reality will affect my view of the best way to live and the proper goals for my life.

Everyone has some ideas about the nature of reality—even if they don't consciously consider the issue. We all carry unconscious background assumptions that shape our thinking and perception of the world. In other words, each of us has our own personal theory on the nature of things, and this guides how we live. Because of this, I devote a lot of time to observing and studying the world around me—so I can try to form as true a picture of reality as I possibly can.

If my theory of reality is warped, my theory of life will be warped, too.

I believe that mind is real and that consciousness and experience are the most important facts about reality. If the universe consisted only of unthinking physical "stuff" (as science tells us), I wouldn't be around to wonder about anything (of course, science wouldn't exist either!). How I live wouldn't matter, because I would have no experience or emotion. What difference would it make? There would be nobody home. What's most important is not that my body exists, but that it thinks and feels. The most important aspect of nature, then, is that, besides physical existence, it is full of experience. Nature is full of gods.

Because mind is the most important fact about nature, and because I am part of nature, I must focus on my mind above all else. The things around me matter only insofar as they affect my mind. None of the things around me are bad or good, except to the degree I allow them to affect my mind.

Mind is most important, and a life principally devoted to cultivating the mind is the best life of all. Because complex thought most distinguishes humans from the rest of nature, to be most human I need to be most thoughtful.

If I live my life without thought, without considering my place in reality, reflecting on the nature of things, I am not living a truly human life. Any animal can live that way, but only a human can live a truly thoughtful life. And so I turn to my mind to find answers to anything. And although it may seem that observing nature directs my attention outward, I am really observing nature's effect on my mind. In reality, the more I look out, the more I look in. I am just nature observing itself.

This ability of the outside world to affect our minds makes life challenging, partly because we are constantly buffeted by a storm of sensations. By their very nature, our minds are restless, constantly projecting themselves onto the outside world. In turn, the world constantly pours into us—into our minds—and so all our knowledge of the "outside" world really occurs within us. I feel this intrusion constantly. Only with great self-discipline can I still my mind; and even then only for short periods, and only if I can find a quiet place where I can temporarily keep the world at bay.

Emotions often erupt without warning, and if we are not careful they can easily sweep us away. Emotions add spice to our lives, but if we let them run wild, we can easily lose ourselves in the storm. We evolved as social animals in a struggle for survival, and emotions developed to help win that struggle. Buried deep within us, left over from our evolutionary past, we all carry desires for safety, comfort, and pleasure. Like many people, I feel their attraction and have spent precious time chasing them. And even though from time to time I have possessed what I desired, those things never really made me happy. In short bursts, possessions have brought me pleasure, but ultimately they left me unfulfilled. I always want more.

Sensual pleasures dull the mind. The more I indulge in such pursuits, the more I lose control of my thoughts. My mind is the most precious part of me; why, then, would I blunt it? The desire for wealth calls out for "more"—always more, more, more. Once I have met my basic needs, what more should I want? And if I go for fame or honors, then I must depend on the opinions and evaluations of others. Why should I put my happiness under their control? If they like me, then I am happy; if they don't, then I am upset. But I don't control their opinions, so how silly to let my happiness depend on them.

And, worst of all, these vain things are so demanding that if I allow my mind to be preoccupied with them, I will have little time left to think of any other good. Desires for fame, wealth, and pleasure becomes all-consuming, eating up my time, filling my mind with useless obsessions. When they become ends in themselves, the objects of our desires become dangerous. If I obsessively seek them, I am lost. However, if I make them means to an end, I can more easily moderate and control them. If I treat them as tools to care for my basic needs, then the danger passes and my mind has time to contemplate more important things.

Happiness is not found outside me. All my emotions happen entirely within my mind. There's no point looking for happiness elsewhere; I can find it only within myself. I value things outside me only insofar as they help me find happiness. That means external objects and events do have some significance and importance. But if I make my happiness depend on those things, then I'll be like a dog chasing its own tail.

Isn't it much more reasonable to work on cultivating happiness directly inside myself? Quite literally, happiness is a state of mind. So the best route to happiness is to learn to control your mind. If you don't control your own mind, you have no control over your own happiness. And if you don't control your own happiness, don't be surprised when you find yourself miserable.

Instead of chasing after things such as money, fame, and power... hoping they will lead to nice, happy, feelings, I should learn to achieve good feelings directly within my own mind. It might seem hard to do this; but, then, how easy is it to acquire money, fame and power – things beyond my control? And once I have them, how long will they last? How long can I count on them being there? And what do I gain once I have them? Money and power don't come easily, and even if they did, they can very easily disappear. When I do get them, sooner or later I find them devoid of value. If I'm going to put so much effort into something, why not focus that effort directly on happiness itself? If I'm going to achieve self-control so I can make money, why not use that self-control to master my thoughts instead of the markets? The things most people think will bring happiness are illusions. In fact, they bring as much—if not more—misery and pain (as many lottery winners can attest).

If you think external possession will make you happy, then by all means go for it. Maybe it really will. But for god's sake, don't puff yourself up with pride when you do. If money, power, and status make you happy, then pride should be the last emotion you feel.

What is Happiness

True happiness is not a bubbly feeling of delight and should not be confused with joy or euphoria. True happiness is, rather, a form of understanding—knowing who you are and your role in nature. It is not pleasure, or jubilation, or comfort. True happiness encompasses many positive and negative emotions. Although it's an emotion, it can also be found through reason. Happiness is a form of peace that comes from understanding and accepting the world as it is. Once you understand nature and your place in it, pride is no longer possible. When pride returns, I lose my understanding and with it my happiness. Pride obscures my true nature and the nature of things around me. When that happens, the struggle for understanding—and therefore happiness—must begin again.

On what, then, does happiness depend? I say it depends on the nature of the things I love. If I love vulgar things, then my mind will be polluted. If I love noble things, then my mind will remain free and pure. The things that surround me are perishable, transient, and empty. They can bring me small pleasures, but I must put them in their proper place. When I try to hold on to them too tightly, when I let my mind obsess over them, I hurt myself and inevitably disturb and damage my mind, blocking out happiness. All things must be judged according to their intrinsic value, appreciated while they're here but not missed when they're gone. The world brings many small pleasures—the feeling of warm sun on my skin, or the smell of cool mist as I walk through a forest; the joys of friendship, and the feeling of accomplishment. But I can truly appreciate these only when my mind is properly focused. If I let myself obsess about my fears and hopes for the future or my feelings for the past, I won't be aware of all of the delights that surround me.

I can be happy if I learn to be simple. The best things in life are easy to get, if I learn to control my desires. Human relationships are the most beautiful gift from the universe and they surround me! A beautiful relationship is free; it costs no money, and asks nothing of me except that I remain open, true, and just. Anyone can have this. The interplay of two minds is a miracle, a marvel of nature that we each exist and can somehow communicate. In the interactions between free minds, we explore new terrains of emotion and reach new levels of understanding and knowledge.

As I look at the things around me, if I don't understand their true nature I can be easily fooled. I have to break things down in my mind, understand their parts and the whole they compose. All possessions made of matter are destined to fall apart. People, too, are destined to decompose. But while we are alive, a miracle happens—the miracle of self-awareness, the most important feature of the world.

The Principles of Happiness

For us, nature's final accomplishment is contemplation, becoming aware, and a way of living in harmony with nature. Make sure, then, that you do not die without having contemplated all these realities . . . will you never realize, then, who you are, why you were born, and what this spectacle is to which you have been admitted?

—Epictetus

What principles can I use to guide my life? Why should I even reflect on any of this?

First, thinking is most evolved in humans, and gives us meaning. To be most human, then, I should spend a lot of time thinking.

Second, minds are the most important entities that exist; and so I should value interactions between minds. To do that, I need to understand as best I can what a mind actually is.

Third, to know how to live I need to understand life and understand myself; so I must study science and philosophy.

If I don't do these things, I'm living on the surface of things, like an unthinking animal.

Control

Some things are in our control and others are not. Things in our control are opinion, pursuit, desire, aversion, and, in a word, whatever are our own actions. Things not in our control are body, property, reputation, command, and, in a word, whatever are not our own actions. The things in our control are by nature free, unrestrained, unhindered; but those not in our control are weak, slavish, restrained, belonging to others. Remember, then, that if you suppose that things which are slavish by nature are also free, and that what belongs to others is your own, then you will be hindered. You will lament, you will be disturbed, and you will find fault both with gods and men. But if you suppose that only to be your own which is your own, and what belongs to others such as it really is, then no one will ever compel you or restrain you. You will find fault with no one or accuse no one. You will do nothing against your will. No one will hurt you, you will have no enemies, and you will not be harmed.

—Epictetus

When I look out at the vastness of the night sky and see innumerable stars, I feel small. Several hundred billion stars populate our galaxy, and hundreds of billions of galaxies exist in the universe, each galaxy with hundreds of billions of stars of its own. These numbers are so mind-blowing as to be impossible to truly comprehend. When we see the ring of stars that surrounds us, we intuitively glimpse the magnitude of the universe and our own infinitesimal size. I imagine everyone feels this at some point. The universe is so large and so old, I am so small, frail, and temporary by comparison. The universal process continues relentlessly and everything slips through my fingers. I can hold on to nothing. Time steadily pushes me along. Yet despite all of this, my emotions are not small. Regardless of how many stars exist, or how small I am, my emotions have a force and power that makes all of that irrelevant. At times my passions overwhelm me with an indescribable intensity. What does it matter how small I am or how big the universe is? Happiness is still the same. Feelings are the same whether experienced by a giant or by a little person.

I have very little control over the things that lie outside me. Nature proceeds on its course, and I can do little about it. I am swept along as time and matter flow through me. Human affairs are convoluted and unpredictable. No matter how powerful one becomes, only a fool thinks he truly controls anything. History is full of examples of the hubris of powerful people who in the end learned how little they actually controlled. Chance exists everywhere. Why, for instance, have I not died of cancer? Why am I this body, here and now, instead of some other body, somewhere else? I find myself in a particular society at a particular point in time, and I can do nothing about that, either.

However, even though I cannot control those external things, I can control my own mind—my opinions, my beliefs, and my desires.

If I make my happiness depend on external things—on other people, on events I believe must happen in order for me to be happy, on things I believe I must own, on a certain status in society I believe I must have—then I'm a fool. I cannot control any of that, only my own thoughts and actions.

If I let my happiness depend on external things, can I ever be free? Would I not be a slave to something else?

> *If you wish your children, and your wife, and your friends to live forever, you are stupid; for you wish to be in control of things which you cannot, you wish for things that belong to others to be your own. So likewise, if you wish your servant to be without fault, you are a fool; for you wish vice to not be vice, but something else. But, if you wish to have your desires undisappointed, this is in your own control. Exercise, therefore, what is in your control. He is the master of every other person who is able to confer or remove whatever that person wishes either to have or to avoid. Whoever, then, would be free, let him wish nothing, let him decline nothing, which depends on others else he must necessarily be a slave.*
>
> *—Epictetus*

To live a beautiful life, I must shape my mind. I must arch my desires toward a worthy goal. I have to learn how to enjoy the things that come my way, regardless of whether I asked for them. Beauty exists in everything; I just need to learn to see it. Nature delights in surprising us. I find myself here, experiencing the world around me right now; I know many others have come before me, and many others will follow. Yet I am never anyone else; I am always me. Why is that? Why doesn't nature allow me to choose whom to be? To get upset over that, of course, would be like getting upset at gravity for always pulling me down rather than floating me up. Reality is a miracle and we understand so little of it. It puts us here, in a certain form with our curious little minds. It sends emotions such as happiness, sadness, and bitterness our way, and we have to somehow make sense of it all. I cannot exert control over reality; I can only weakly influence the unfolding of the process. I perceive the wonder that surrounds me . . . and welcome it. My body and mind must obey the laws of nature, and must find a way through the turmoil of society. Yet whenever I give up the desire for control and learn to appreciate this great show a deep pleasure awaits me.

When I allow my desires to take over, I set myself up for disappointment. Nature does not promise me riches or comfort, power or fame. Why should I allow those desires, no matter how small, to take hold of my mind? If I align my desires with nature, then my mind will be pure and free. If I always remember the true nature of things, I will enjoy them when they're around and I will not miss them when they are gone. I will not obsess over things or expect more than nature has promised. I will not allow success to puff me up with pride or disappointments to crush me.

If I continue to delve deep inside my own mind, the wonder of the universe awaits. In brief flashes of inspiration, I can see the unity and interconnectedness of all things.

> *Nothing is so productive of greatness of mind as the ability to examine systematically and truthfully each thing we encounter in life, and to see these things in such a way as to comprehend the nature of the Cosmos, and what sort of benefits such things possess for both the Whole and for humans. . . . This thing or circumstance that now gives me an impression: What is it? What is it made of? How long will it last? And, most important, what quality does it require of me, such as gentleness, courage, honesty, faith, simplicity, independence, and the like?*
>
> *—Marcus Aurelius*

> *Remember that following desire promises the attainment of that of which you are desirous; and aversion promises the avoiding of that to which you are averse. However, he who fails to obtain the object of his desire is disappointed, and he who incurs the object of his aversion wretched. If, then, you confine your aversion to those objects only which are contrary to the natural use of your faculties, which you have in your own control, you will never incur anything to which you are averse. But if you are averse to sickness, or death, or poverty, you will be wretched. Remove aversion, then, from all things that are not in our control. But, for the present, totally suppress desire: for, if you desire any of the things which are not in your own control, you must necessarily be disappointed; and of those which are, and which it would be laudable to desire, nothing is yet in your possession. Use only the appropriate actions of pursuit and avoidance; and even these lightly, and with*

gentleness and reservation.

—Epictetus

Action and Inaction

My lack of control over the wider world, however, is no cause for despair. I am an odd type of creature, active and passive at the same time. Sometimes I am capable of great freedom, other times I am swept up by forces beyond my control. Nature is in control, but I am part of nature. In the same way that an individual ant influences the behavior of the colony and, in turn, is itself influenced by the colony, I influence nature but am also influenced by her.

This practice of controlling my emotions and understanding the true nature of my freedom is not an argument for passivity. Rather, I must understand my nature so I can guide my thoughts and actions toward things worthy of my attention. If I allow myself to desire things contrary to my nature, I will inevitably suffer. If, instead, in each moment I maintain awareness of the true nature of things (including my own), my mind will harmonize with its surroundings and I will be at peace.

What Use is Status?

The emotions I feel seem to come of their own volition. Most people desire things and they don't even really know why. Maybe evolution programmed these desires into me or I picked them up accidentally from the culture I happened to be born into. Most people believe that acting on their desires will bring them happiness. They believe that if they can fulfill their desires, then they will be satisfied. If you are hungry, you eat. If you are tired, you sleep. If you do not feel important, you fight for status. Such natural desires initiate most human actions. If you feel you want something, you go get it.

Most people want money, not because money itself is useful but because money will allow them to increase their status. How many people desire to be rich so they can keep the lifestyle they already have?

Most desires come from the craving for status—the root of much human weakness. The basics of life are easily met, but rarely are these enough for most people. Usually, we want nice things only because they increase our status. Some people want flashy cars not because they have any inherent value, but because of what they imagine other people will think of them as they drive around.

Look inside at what drives you and what fills your daydreams. Notice if social status dominates your fantasies. Is a 10,000 square-foot house really more comfortable than a 2,000 square-foot house? Do designer clothes last longer, feel better, or provide more warmth than mass-market clothing found in cheap stores? Is there really such a difference in quality? If you buried a Honda and a BMW of the same size, and let thousands of years go by so that all cultural references would be lost, do you think that future archaeologists would be able to figure out which was the higher status car? You might argue that one accelerates better than the other, one has a bigger engine, better brakes, wood and leather interior. Yet not so long ago, the most desirable cars were slow. Think back to the Cadillacs of the 1950s, 60s, and 70s. The modern attractiveness of performance is purely cultural; not so long ago people didn't prioritize performance. Why should leather and wood interiors be considered better and not more primitive than modern plastics?

Our technology has almost entirely erased the quality difference between the mass market and the high end. Yet people still want what the culture decides is high status. Almost no meaningful difference exists in the lifestyle of an average middle-class person and a billionaire in terms of comfort or longevity. We all have the same computers and phones, the same clothing, and essentially the same cars and houses. Even the most modest home will have temperature control, insulation, electricity, TV and Internet service, and other comforts of modern life. Billionaires just have more toys and more exotic vacations.

If we had evolved to desire material comfort, wouldn't we all be happy by now? Wouldn't these desires be coming to an end? Yet we don't see that because we didn't evolve to want material comfort. We evolved to want to dominate our local social group. People want status, simply because we're primates. Having high status brings real evolutionary advantages. It gives animals a better selection of mates and better access to food and shelter. We are descended from apes who, for millions of years, fought and killed for high status. High status enabled them to spread their genes better than low-status rivals. We've inherited those genes and the desires they code.

But these desires don't make us happy. They help us survive. Evolution designs survival machines, not happiness machines. Our desires evolved over long periods to help us win the struggle for survival and reproduction. Our ancestors wielded status as a weapon to help them eat and mate better than low-status apes. Today, we humans indulge in these same desires without thinking because we automatically follow our instincts. Many of us simply assume without question that getting the things we want will make us happy. For most of us, this deeply ingrained belief remains mostly unconscious.

We all know people who seem to get what they want, but still aren't happy. That's because they are not chasing happiness itself, but rather possessions they believe will lead to happiness. They habitually follow instincts designed to help them outbreed others, not instincts that will make them happy. Why should we expect happiness to come from external things? Happiness exists only in our minds; only there will we find it.

We have little control over external things, and even less over how other people think. However, we do have a lot of control over how we think. Because most people allow happiness to depend on things they don't control, happiness remains forever beyond reach. It depends on chance, or on other people's opinions. Much better to control your own opinions, your own emotions, your own mind, as the path to happiness.

The Art of Living

> *Philosophy does not claim to secure for us anything outside of our control. Otherwise it would be taking on matters that do not concern it. For as wood is the material of the carpenter, and marble that of the sculptor, so each individual's own life is the material of the art of living.*
>
> *—Epictetus*

Life is difficult because it requires judgment. It requires the exercise of reason in order to live well . . . something very hard to do.

Life is the gift of nature, but beautiful living is the gift of wisdom.

– Greek saying

In order to live well, we must make reason a habit. Throughout the day, as I go about my business, I feel a constant surge of emotions. Sometimes they seem positive, sometimes negative. It is so easy to be swept away by emotions, to jump on them as they arise, and ride them to the end. But, if I seek happiness, this is exactly what I can't allow myself to do.

I control some things in life but not others. The big events that happen lie beyond my control. When I feel like things simply happen to me and I allow myself to see those things as either good or bad, I am lost. At that point, I am no longer in control of my happiness. If I believe what happened is "good," then I am happy; and if it's "bad," then I am sad. But if I allow myself to think like this, chance wins. Good or bad does not lie in that thing or event itself. It is neither good nor bad. Good or bad occurs only in my mind. The things that happen in life are just events, just nature doing what it naturally does. Events simply happen, following the inexorable logic and laws of reality. Only my reactions are good or bad.

If something happens to me and I allow it to make me angry, then that is bad. If something happens and I use it to increase my understanding, increase my knowledge, increase my serenity, then that is good. But the thing itself is neither bad nor good; only what I do with it. Every moment presents an opportunity for me to improve, but I have to seize it!

Good and bad exist only in my mind, which filters everything I experience.

Men are disturbed, not by the things which happen, but by the opinions about the things.: for example, death is nothing terrible, for if it were, it would have seemed so to Socrates; for the opinion about death, that it is terrible, is the terrible thing. When, then, we are impeded or disturbed or grieved, let us never blame others, but ourselves, that is, our opinions. It is the act of an ill-instructed man to blame others for his own bad condition; it is the act of one who has begun to be instructed, to lay the blame on himself; and of one whose instruction is completed, neither to blame another, nor himself.

—Epictetus

Things do happen, but they affect me only as much as I choose to let them. I choose what I value and what I spend my time thinking about. It's not easy to achieve the level of control necessary to be at peace with nature, but it's not impossible either.

I choose what to dwell on, what to think about, what's important to me. I choose what to worry about, what to enjoy. I can spend my time reading tabloids and wasting time, or studying important things. I can worry about status, money, and attractiveness, or I can spend time contemplating nature and all its beauty.

The physical world simply *is*, I can't change much of it. Human nature simply *is*, too. Nature does not consult me before it acts. Neither do other people. Other people choose to live their lives according to their own desires. I cannot let that affect me more than is proper.

Human nature is difficult to conquer, and most of us will succumb to the emotions that flood our minds. But I don't aim for perfection; just to continuously improve.

Happiness and Reason

Perhaps the universe does not care whether we are happy. But then how strange that emotions should exist at all. Why should the universe create beings that can experience pain? Why do we not all live in an earthly paradise? Why should the nature of reality be such that struggle seems necessary? Perhaps we just don't understand, because we don't see things from the cosmic perspective. But we don't experience daily life from the cosmic perspective. We experience life from the viewpoint of a fragile, mortal being. And from this viewpoint, happiness and pain are quite real.

Given all this, if a living thing seeks happiness that goal must align with whatever the universe allows. Does it make sense to look for something fleeting and difficult to achieve? A truly rational approach would acknowledge that misery is as much a part of life as comfort.

However, we cannot stop desiring happiness. So we need to ask: What kind of happiness is it rational to desire? We tend to view happiness as a positive, bubbly emotion, a slightly subdued version of joy. However, the universe appears to be uninterested in our happiness. Misery is just as likely. History is full of strife and suffering as well as beautiful achievements. The error is not in desiring happiness, but in misunderstanding the meaning of happiness and confusing it with something else. Happiness worth desiring must be found through direct experience. True happiness is the serenity of understanding nature.

Because of evolution, living things have desires and impulses, which naturally pull us toward the objects of our desire. Whenever I experience this pulling sensation, I view the desire as inherently good. If I don't reflect on the source of my feelings, I end up unconsciously believing that fulfilling my desires will increase my happiness.

Desires have many sources—culture, personal history, evolutionary heritage, life's contingencies, including the accident of our birth. These desires do not necessarily lead to real happiness.

If I unreflectively follow my natural desires and instincts, I will be easily led astray. Nature has not promised me true knowledge; I must find that for myself. Such knowledge will not simply fall into my lap. How can I believe that life will naturally lead me to happiness when my desires were not designed for my happiness?

Nature will not fulfill my base desires. I cannot avoid misery and pain, and I know that happiness cannot lie in trying to avoid them. Nature decides all that.

And so, I face a conundrum: A common view of happiness equates it with getting what we want; but an honest view of the universe shows that getting what we want isn't possible. We want to avoid pain, but we will still feel it. We want everyone to love us, but not everyone will. Perhaps, with luck, a few people will experience little pain or sadness. But would that really be luck? Would never experiencing struggle be a worthwhile life? I can't shake the feeling that happiness is good, and I chase it instinctively. What we commonly believe to be happiness, however, is hardly ever worthy of the name.

True happiness is not comfort or the absence of pain. It results from insight into the true nature of reality and a vision of what is eternal. It arises from understanding who and what you are and your role in the larger scheme of life. It acknowledges that pain and struggle are part of happiness, just as much as joy. Happiness comes with insight into the unity of all things, realizing we are part of the one process at work everywhere. This insight binds my mind to the rest of nature.

Intellectual and Emotional Knowledge

Knowledge comes in two forms: intellectual and emotional. Intellectual knowledge is theory. Emotional knowledge comes from experience, from living and feeling the truth of things.

In the end, the difference between the two is merely a matter of degree. At root, all knowledge arises from experience, from feeling. Intellectual knowledge, by contrast, is a more superficial stage of knowledge. In order to truly know something, I must feel it deep within my bones. In the same way that I exercise my body, I have to exercise my mind in order to convert intellectual knowledge into embodied knowledge. Doing so, I can transform things I know superficially into things I know deep down inside.

You may know that getting punched in the face hurts. You may know a lot about nerve cells and how they work. You may know a lot about the force generated by a punch and how that interacts with the nerve cells of your body to generate pain. This is intellectual knowledge. But is this the same as knowing the feeling of a punch striking your cheek?

Experience changes everything.

Likewise, all arguments about life and how to live remain just words until you actually experience life yourself. You have to go through the struggle. You have to have real doubt about yourself, about your reason for existing, about your goals in life. Intellectual knowledge differs significantly from knowledge gained through direct experience. We need both. First we must understand why things are the way they are and why we should live a certain way. Then we must feel those reasons so deeply that no arguments are needed anymore to convince us of their truth.

Life offers no shortcuts; but over time you may develop the ability to truly learn from the experiences of others. When you study nature and philosophy, you can experience things in your mind that you wouldn't experience otherwise. Even though such knowledge comes from books and abstract observations, it can slowly change you as well. Some knowledge starts out as purely intellectual, but through contemplation it can transform into emotional experiences, helping us to see things in a new light. After all, if you decided to become a physicist, would you just start scribbling equations down or would you first study what's already been discovered? And if you wanted to become a lawyer, would you just walk into a courtroom and hold forth in front of a judge or would you first go to law school and prepare?

Likewise, when it comes to the art of living, shouldn't we first seek instruction? What's more important than knowing how to live? We get no extra points for making things up as we go along. Many wise people came before us, and dedicated their lives to figuring out what life means. I think it wise to study them before I go off and invent my own way of living. I should learn from their mistakes and their discoveries.

Unknowing

As much as I try to understand nature and explain my beliefs about ultimate reality, I do not think I can actually make any true statements about it. Reality transcends language and defies final descriptions. When it comes to explaining what happens around us, human language ultimately fails. We can point to things here and there and make statements that partially illuminate understanding, but true knowledge comes without words or thought. When I speak to myself silently in my mind, using words and images, I approach truth but never reach it.

At first, only partial and sporadic, nature's truth typically comes as an unpredictable realization—a flash, a vision, an insight into the true essence of things. Through contemplation, I can stretch these moments out longer and longer. With practice, I can have more control over when these moments of clarity arrive, but the process still relies as much on a burst of inspiration as on systematic reflection.

More through a kind of ineffable unknowing, we can see through the outer forms of phenomena and peer into their true nature. Only by stripping concepts from my mind and ignoring the constant stream of thoughts can I catch glimpses of truth.

I sometimes picture it this way: a large block of wood stands in front of me hiding a shape I want to make visible. In order to reveal that hidden shape, I must cut away the wood that obscures it, making its essence visible for everyone else, too. Similarly, as the ancient Greek philosopher Heraclitus said: "Nature loves to hide." In flashes of inspiration, I can cut through outer forms and see the inner essence of things. However, to communicate what I see to someone else, I have to use language. Unfortunately, unlike carving a block of wood, I cannot simply chip away at the surface of reality to reveal metaphysical truths. Language can point the way, but it can never take us there.

Nature exists both inside and outside everything, without ever being enclosed or excluded by anything. It remains forever obscured by innumerable physical forms and non-physical mental concepts. Truth remains hidden from me until, like a diamond cutting through steel, I can let my direct experience slice through obscurity. This process is unknowing.

In order to approach ultimate knowledge, I must unlearn everything else. In those moments of clarity, all words cease, all concepts dissolve, and I simply perceive. Only direct experience yields pure and lucid understanding.

> *As long as I am this or that, or have this or that, I am not all things and I have not all things. Become pure till you neither are nor have either this or that; then you are omnipresent and, being neither this nor that, are all things*
>
> *—Meister Eckhart*

Mind

Mind or consciousness—the ability to feel, to be aware, and to choose—is the most mysterious thing in nature. It's the only reason I know I'm alive, yet awareness can be so bittersweet. Emotion can sweep me out to sea like a forceful tide; or send me tumbling down a mountain cliff, grasping at anything I can.

Nature created me. I evolved through the filter of natural selection, which designed me to be a survival machine, not a happiness machine. From the first stirrings of life, billions of years ago, an unbroken line of animals has successfully reproduced in order to create me, from the simplest bacteria through innumerable ancestors until I finally arrive. This lineage of ancestors survived to reproduce across billions of years—and here I am! Had anyone of them failed, I would not be. Nevertheless, ninety-nine percent of species that ever existed have gone extinct. Just imagine how many individuals have come and gone without leaving any heirs! Yet I exist. Whatever my ancestors did must have been very good for survival.

But how does that knowledge help me be happy here and now? If I understand why I feel the things I do, I can put them in their proper place. If I understand where my desires come from, I can value them properly.

Every organism has its own natural "essence" or essential nature. For example, like all other animals, a mouse naturally explores its surroundings. Curiosity helps it find food and shelter. Because of its innate curiosity, if I put a mouse in a maze, it will naturally run back and forth, exploring openings and dead-ends. It won't stop to think about why it's there, what the maze is, or whether it makes any sense for it to probe its surroundings. Mice have survived and reproduced by naturally exploring their immediate environment, finding food and places to hide, so that's what it will do if you put one in a maze.

Like other primates, humans, too, have natural drives—for example, to seek status, for much the same reasons. Being a high-status member of a social group helps a primate survive and reproduce. But there's a big difference between a mouse and a human: unlike mice, we have the ability to reflect. We have more free will than any other animal.

Look at how most people live today: we have much more material wealth than our ancestors. Although hundreds of millions still go to bed hungry every night, most people in Western countries have access to food, shelter, and medicine. In many cases, even the poorest among us have TVs, microwaves, and cell phones. We live in the richest historical era, by far. Yet the struggle for status has not abated. Despite almost universal access to modern comforts and conveniences, most people do not feel content with what they have. The rat-race continues and everyone wants *more, more, more* . . .

In today's world, we don't need high social status in order to survive. Status does not make us happy. That kind of fleeting pleasure conditions us to chase after it continuously; and when we get it, we soon discover it's worthless. Happiness does not come from external possessions or social status; it comes from somewhere else, somewhere deep inside each of us. To achieve and maintain high-status primates must be aggressive, anxious, paranoid—constantly on the lookout for threats to dominance. Why, then, should we expect status to bring us lasting happiness?

However, nature has designed us to want status; so what can we do about it? Can we fight nature? We don't need to; we just need to use other natural abilities—such as free will. We can reflect; we can contemplate. We don't have to follow through on our instincts like a mouse or a monkey. Most of the time, we can ignore our basic survival instincts because we don't really need to act on them in this day and age. We can, instead, focus on cultivating true happiness.

Status, envy, greed. Survival, survival, survival. What do they do for me now? Nothing but make me anxious and unhappy. When an impression strikes me, I must make sure I analyze it carefully: What is this? Why am I feeling it? Should I accept or reject it? I have that power, I must use it.

The impressions that come to me through my senses merely report what's going on in the world around me. I don't need to judge them as "this is good, that is bad." I can trick myself into believing that externals are good or bad; but if I do I quickly lose control of my own happiness. When my happiness depends on something external, something over which I have no control, then when the situation changes, my state of happiness will change, too. Why give such power to things we don't control? Better to be like a rock in the pounding surf, letting the waves of sensations and emotions crash around me, while I remain undisturbed.

Experiences make life worth living. Without experience, we would never know we're alive at all! Mental events—such as sensations, perceptions, thoughts, emotions, choices—provide the rich texture of life, all our little (and great) pleasures and disappointments, all the joys and pain and everything in between that make us human. However, I must be careful about which emotions or thoughts I dwell on. I don't aim to eradicate all emotions from my life; instead, I practice watching them come and go—enjoying them all, the good and the bad. Doing so, I experience the peace and understanding that constitute true happiness, and have a deeper sense of my place in the universe. I learn to accept nature as it is, not as I wish it to be. Living with this awareness, I cultivate virtues—such as acting well toward others, contemplating life, being grateful for my existence—not resenting the fact that the laws of nature didn't give me what I happen to believe they should have.

Happiness that grows from within does not shift in response to changes of fortune or the whims of society. Because it comes from inside me, I alone must take responsibility for my state of happiness.

What is the Ideal Life?

Most people seem to believe that being born rich is a blessing. They idolize the rich and famous—who appear to have an easy life. Perhaps being born into poverty is truly a curse, although I suspect even that may not necessarily be true. As long as you have food and shelter, happiness is well within reach. But is being born into wealth such a blessing?

At times in life, I've had more money than the vast majority of people in history ever had. But this didn't make me happy. My moments or periods of happiness did not arise because of my wealth. People born into wealth and an easy life tend to live in a bubble of unreality, isolated from the truth of nature. If we are not careful, comfort and affluence dull the mind. In order to pierce the veil of nature, understand its secrets, and respond appropriately to its unfolding, our minds must be razor sharp. If you love truth, you will want to live a real, authentic life, even beyond your comfort zone. Given the power of imagination, we have the blessing and the curse of being able to choose: to live in fantasy or in contact with the reality of nature. From time immemorial, happiness and sadness have occurred in everyone's life, and will continue to do so. Life is full of misery and joy, and try as we might, we cannot isolate ourselves from that. Trying to avoid the "shadow" side of life will only make you weak, ignorant, and ultimately foolish. Being born into wealth, never having to struggle, is nothing to envy.

> *We take pity on the blind and lame, why don't we pity people who are blind and lame in respect of what matters most?*
>
> *—Epictetus*

He believes that the misfortune of the wise man is better than the prosperity of the fool

—Diogenes Laertius, The Life of Epicurus

If mind is the most important thing in the universe, then developing your mind is the most important thing you can do. And how can you do that if you cut yourself off from nature? You have to live in the world and all that it entails. Struggle is part of nature and part of life. You have to feel it. A life of comfort is nothing to covet; that would be a life of weakness and ignorance that blunts the spirit—the exact opposite of what you want.

When I was younger, I often thought that being born into wealth and fame would be desirable. It would have given me, right from the start what so many people work for their whole lives.

Experience is a cruel teacher, but sometimes necessary. In the same way a doctor might need to prescribe a bitter medicine to cure a disease, life must sometimes challenge us in order for us to grow. I've experienced setbacks just like everyone else. At first, I pitied myself, feeling unlucky. I felt that life was unfair and unjust. But as I considered it more, I realized that a life of affluence and leisure is no blessing. Easy success is nothing to desire; it dulls the mind and thinking becomes sluggish and shallow. As I progressed, each successive blow from fate affected me less and less and I soon found I had nothing to fear from the things I used to worry about. The more I toiled, the sharper my thinking became. The less I allowed myself to be fooled by my desires, the deeper I penetrated into nature. Eventually, this developed into a love of knowledge as an end in itself, a duty to instruct myself and fortify my mind.

Difficult times force us to question and look for truth. When we feel comfortable, we can all-too easily let time waste away and gain nothing. Struggle brings out the best in us and is the best defense against ignorance.

I no longer envy people born into an easy life. What a waste to live your entire life in a fog of ignorance, blind to the reality around you. As difficult as it may be sometimes, I prefer knowledge and all of the initial discomfort and anguish it can bring. Knowledge can be troubling, it does not let us hide behind fluffy little clouds and rainbows. Knowledge carries with it melancholy, but also cheer. It carries gloom and also joy. Ultimately, knowledge develops into understanding, and without understanding it is impossible to exercise good judgment or live well.

To desire riches and fame is to ignore the boundless universe and see only the tiny part in front of us. Allowing such desires, we willingly put on blinders, separate ourselves from the rest of creation, and miss the wondrous reality that surrounds us. When we strive for comfort and riches, we exchange a life of freedom, of wide-open expanses, of mystery and astonishment, for a vulgar and base existence of petty meaninglessness. Nature's beauty always remains open and ready for us to accept and participate in it. Life is beautiful, and simple. We alone can complicate it and turn it into something low and unworthy.

> *But will you let mere fame distract you? Turn your gaze to the quick forgetfulness of all things, the abyss of the ages on either side of this present moment, and the empty echo of praise, the transitory quality and lack of judgment on the part of those who praise, and the tiny area in which all this is confined. For the entire earth is only a mere point in the universe, and what a small corner of the earth is our dwelling place; and in that place, see how few and of what sort are the people who celebrate you!*
>
> *—Marcus Aurelius*

> *The man who pants after praise and yearns to "make history" forgets that those who remember him will die soon after he goes to his grave, as will those who succeed the first generation of them that praise him, until after passing from one generation to the next, through many generations, the bright flame of his memory will flutter, fade, and go out. But what if those who praise you never died, and they sang your praises forever? What difference would that make? That the praise will do nothing for you dead isn't my point. What will it do for you now that you're still alive, except perhaps offer a means to some other end? Meanwhile, you neglect nature's means of achieving the same ends directly while worrying about you'll be remembered after you're dead.*
>
> *— Marcus Aurelius*

The Lives of Others

If you see someone just sitting there, you have no idea what's going on in his or her head—obvious, you might think, but it's worth reflecting on. For instance, you may see someone who looks homeless and not give him a moment's thought. However, he could be much more than his appearance. Take for example, Diogenes the Cynic, an ancient Greek philosopher, who lived that way. Without knowing what was going on inside his head, you might have mistaken him for a troubled vagrant.

Some might say that if he lived like a vagrant, then he was a vagrant. Sometimes that's the case, but sometimes not. He was homeless for a very deep reason. In order to be truly free, he had to separate himself from everything else. Few can live such a radical life. But what separated Diogenes from a common transient? Only how he used his mind.

Two different people can appear to be doing exactly the same thing, but inside their minds they may be worlds apart. While their actions might appear the same, depending on how and what they think, the significance and value of their actions could be very different.

Because we can't know what is going on in other people's minds, we should not be too quick to judge. We need to keep this in mind as we go about our daily lives. Each one of us popped into existence in a certain time and place; we each need to make a living and do all of the practical things that everyone does. But what really matters is what happens inside our minds.

When your inner life is well ordered, it will eventually show in your outer life, too. But if your inner life lacks order, whatever you do will just be a cheap facade.

> *For sheep don't throw up the grass to show the shepherds how much they have eaten; but, inwardly digesting their food, they outwardly produce wool and milk. Thus, therefore, do you likewise not show philosophical ideas to the unlearned, but the actions produced by them after they have been digested.*
>
> *—Epictetus*

What is a Typical Human Life?

People are born into a particular time and place. From the standpoint of any individual, the circumstances of their birth appear random. Why should I be born in this particular place, at this particular time? Billions of people are alive now and billions have existed before me. Each one of them experienced a totally different set of events. Why do I experience what I do? Given the mental and physical nature of matter, as it forms itself into persons each of us becomes aware of our self. This self-awareness might seem mysterious to us, although it is an inescapable consequence of the natural processes at work. But this briefest of explanations does not explain anything. It is merely a statement of observation. The strangeness of the particular conscious stream I experience is unique to me; you must experience your own stream of consciousness for yourself. The wonder of it all cannot be satisfactorily explained by making trivial observations.

Given the natural processes that lead to the formation of planets, life, and eventually thinking individuals, each person has a unique set of experiences and sensory impressions. We all see and hear certain things, in a certain sequence, different from everyone else. Because of this, each one of us has a unique body of knowledge. Each person has a unique perspective on reality that cannot be adequately conveyed in words. In this sense, each of us remains totally isolated, because no one else can climb inside anybody else's body and experience what they experience. We attempt to overcome this through language, art, and shared experiences that we imagine affect others as they affect us. We spend much of our lives trying to overcome this isolation, trying to connect to others so they can feel what we feel and vice versa.

Each of us inherits certain modes of thinking depending on the particular culture we happen to be born into. We can change our thinking, but it requires much effort—and, as a result, too few do. These cultural modes of thinking take root at such an early age they are rarely ever noticed when we grow up. The larger physical and cultural background of my life creates a whole host of invisible assumptions that color my view of everything if I don't examine them.

What, then, is the ideal life? Had I been born into an 11th century Mayan culture, or an Asian tribe in 7,000 BCE, how different would my inner life be? What if I had been born a German woman in 1902?

Each of us must decide how we want to live. We must decide what we value, what we will spend time contemplating, and what is most important to us. The accident of my birth propels me in a certain direction with some momentum, but I must still agree to continue that path. If another path opens for me, it is up to me to take it.

A Message Into the Past

I often wonder about the kind of life I would like to have led had I been born in the past. Would I have wanted to become a successful merchant or a brave soldier? Had I been born in, say, Greece in the year 278 CE, would I have aimed to be a top politician or a skilled lawyer? From my current vantage point, what would I consider to be a successful life had I lived back then?

When I read now about people from ancient Greece, I'm not impressed by that period's best olive-oil merchants or most successful politicians. I don't really care about the skills that people had in competing in the markets of the time or in the political arena. That economy, their political environment—their whole world—has long since disappeared. I am impressed, however, when I read of someone who understood the rue nature of reality and their role in it; someone who behaved with grace, who was just and honest, who thought deeply about life and how to behave. The skills it takes to succeed in daily life do, of course, have a certain importance. But their effectiveness belongs to a particular place and time. By contrast, knowledge of the true nature of things remains valid for all time and helps in all situations. Disciplined contemplation of life is truly valuable, not merely an arbitrary or transient good.

I imagine that had I been born a plains Indian in North America in 1,000 BCE, I would have had a particular conception of "the good life" specific to that era and community. Born into that environment and culture, I would have developed certain beliefs and assumptions—probably without question. And had I been born a Mayan in the year 706 CE, I would have had a different conception of the good life, influenced by that time and society. Likewise had I been born in Renaissance Venice or ancient Japan, my life would have been shaped by that time and place. But here I am, a Westerner, living in the 21st century, surrounded by people who obviously have their own specific modern conceptions of "the good life." Perhaps they don't say it explicitly, perhaps they don't even think of it very much, but by their actions I can surmise what they believe the good life to be.

I assume all cultural beliefs share universal themes—products of our deep evolutionary past. For example, as discussed earlier, the desire for status is strong in all of us, a remnant of our earlier mammalian forebears. Although status probably meant different things in different times and places, some form of social status has always been highly-prized.

Experience has taught me that most of things I have desired are meaningless, empty, and of little true value. I picked up those desires randomly, from the accident of my birth and my evolutionary heritage. When I got those things, they brought me little happiness, and when I lost them, I didn't miss them much. Unfortunately, I had to learn this lesson the hard way; perhaps there is no other way to learn this type of lesson.

When I read something that someone wrote centuries ago, I often imagine the author sitting at his desk writing. What did the room look like? What shapes, sounds, colors, and smells made up his world? What did he believe about the universe? What did life mean to him? Did he pray? And for what? We don't have to read things written too far back to realize that the world that writer inhabited has completely disappeared. Everyone alive then is now dead; and like the dead authors themselves, everyone they knew is also long gone. Their towns have disappeared, casualties of time, swallowed by the earth and the activities of men. In some cases, even their religion may be no more. Whatever they believed has been forgotten. And all we know of those people and their world—a world that must have seemed so alive and so real to them—are fragments of writings or the whispers of archaeological digs.

History is full of the remnants of past minds. We are left with just hints and suggestions of what their lives were like, the events, people and places they experienced. We must now rely only on shreds of evidence that vaguely point to the experiences that lit up their lives. We have no "fossil record" of past minds. The closest we have are their writings and other artifacts, expressions of their beliefs, hopes, and dreams. For example, read the speeches of Demosthenes from the 4th century BCE as he railed against the Macedonian tyrant Philip II and his conquests of the Greek city states. You can feel the fear of imminent invasion and uncertainty about what to do. Yet who knows anything about that now? What must have seemed so real to the Athenians alive then seems so unreal and distant to us now. Their fears have been replaced by words on scraps of paper, the residue of experiences now lost in time.

In the end, Phillip did attack and the Athenians fell in battle. But no-one experiences this now. We can only imagine ourselves into their skins. Where did those feelings go? Where is that reality now? A world that was palpably alive has now disappeared. How ironic that the monument the Athenians set up after their loss to Phillip II at the Battle of Chaeronea in 338 BCE should read:

> *Time, the all-surveying deity of all kinds of affairs for mortals/ Be a messenger to all men of our sufferings / How striving to save the sacred land of Greece/ We died on the famed plains of Boeotia.*

Now it's just another obscure and long-lost historical artifact, interesting mainly to specialists. I'm sure it meant a lot to them. It expressed their concerns about life and death, the destruction or survival of their way of life, but no one cares now. The entire world those people inhabited is long gone. Their world has been replaced over and over by new worlds, new people and new experiences of life. The ceaseless churning of time has consumed their thoughts and emotions, and from those remnants we now create entirely new experiences.

When I read something like the speeches of Demosthenes or the letters of someone from 2,000 years ago, I often ask myself: if I could send a message back in time, what would I tell them? What do I know that they don't? Could I enlighten them? Could I tell them the meaning of life and the secrets of the universe? Could I give them the secret to happiness? Could I, who lives in such an advanced age and with the benefit of thousands of years of hindsight, tell them anything truly valuable they couldn't discover for themselves?

What message would I send to a 13-year old Mayan boy, or a 35-year old Native American woman from 5,000 years ago? What would I tell an Athenian barber in 338 BCE or a Byzantine Roman from 850 CE or a Balkan slave of the 2ND century CE? Is there some nugget of wisdom I could impart, some true fact that would hold for all of them and be of some value? Is the gulf of time and culture too wide and deep to overcome?

I know only one thing with certainty that perhaps they didn't: that their world would eventually and inevitably disappear. Perhaps they knew this intellectually, everyone does on some level, but who really feels death? Who feels the reality of the immense passages of time that will wipe away everything around them? Who truly believes that buildings made of solid stone will crumble, that new trees will sprout through the earth and transform the landscape, that billions of people will be born, live, and die after them?

I would tell them that from my perspective in time, everything that surrounded them has now disappeared. In my time, nothing remains of what they saw every day. The universal process has continued, wiping away everything, rejuvenating the land over and over again. Such a perspective tells us not to worry about the small nuisances of life, not to worry about setbacks or successes. Don't worry about status or fame or riches. No one alive now cares; and even if someone from my time did care, what good would that to people back then? I would have to tell them:

"You will disappear and everyone you know will disappear. Don't despair at this, it really is true even though you may not feel it in your bones. But this is no reason to be sad; it's simply the nature of things. Everything changes, everything disappears. The process continues. Enjoy the moments you have, focus on your mind and the experience of living now. Look for happiness now, inside yourself now. Time will devour you and everyone you know. If you can't find happiness in your own mind, you will not find it outside. Apply yourself to the present moment—because nothing else is truly yours. The past is gone and the future has not yet come; only the present exists for you. Focus on the beauty of the simple things around you, on the joy of existing, on your relationships, and pay attention to the minds—the desires, fears, joys, beliefs, emotions, and thoughts—of the people that surround you. Contemplate the wondrous nature of reality, the miraculous spectacle that envelops you. That is all that truly matters."

> *The seed of God is in us. Given an intelligent and hard-working farmer, it will thrive and grow up to God, whose seed it is; and accordingly its fruits will be God-nature. Pear seeds grow into pear trees, nut seeds into nut trees, and God seed into God*
>
> *—Meister Eckhart*

> *Let me tell you how you should regard me: as one no less happy or cheerful than when his fortunes were best. And they are indeed*

now best, as my mind, free from all other occupation, has leisure for its own tasks, sometimes delighting in less serious studies, sometimes, in its passion for the truth, rising to the contemplation of its own nature and that of the universe. It strives to know, first, the lands of the earth and where they lie, then the laws which govern the surrounding sea with its recurring motions of ebb and flow; then it examines all that, filled with terrors, lies between heaven and earth, this expanse disturbed by thunder, lightning, blasts of winds, and the rain and snow and hail that fall upon our heads; then, once it has ranged over the lower spaces, it bursts through to the heights, and enjoys the beautiful spectacle of divine things, and, remembering its own immortality, it proceeds to all that has been and will come into being throughout all time's ages.

—Seneca

The Forms of Nature

Nature takes on many different forms, both supra-personal: transcendent, abstract, above and beyond all human understanding; and also intensely personal: our bodies and minds, the people and things around us. Nature exists everywhere and we are shards of the one true nature, self-reflective, seeing in ourselves a universal nature that is at once so present and so hidden.

At times I focus on nature's supra-personal aspect, the infinitely extended reality that eludes all my attempts to grasp it with my mind. I highly value this because it shows me glimpses of the ultimate truth and that nature to which I will return when I die. But at times the supra-personal can be too abstract. My daily life is filled with all the worries and pleasures of a finite person, existing in a particular place and time. During these times, focusing on the personal aspect of nature holds more value for me. Nature takes on the forms of persons, animals, landscapes, thoughts and emotions, and all the things that affect me on an intimate level. Reality is both near and far, present and hidden, love and detachment.

The Nature of the Things We Love

Because consciousness is real, because it is the seat of all experience, thought, and emotion, consciousness should be the focus of my existence. The things that surround me are perishable, transient, ephemeral—just like my thoughts and my self. I love the things I perceive and experience but I have to love them for the right reasons and to love only what is true in them. In themselves, those things are neither good nor bad, except insofar as they affect my mind. If I love them purely for their temporary forms, then I am setting myself up for trouble. Those forms will disappear and when they do, I will feel pain at their passing. The reality that surrounds me is beautiful because of its universal nature *and* the temporary forms it takes on. Universal nature simply *is* change. The temporary forms are the waves on the surface of the ocean. Do I love the ocean or do I love the waves? What difference is there?

The infinite and the universal creates the temporary and the transient. When I focus my mind on this, I can love the temporary forms and delight in them, but not obsess over them because I keep their true nature in mind.

The universe is enveloped in everything. Everything is full of gods. Everything is the flowering of reality. The sea itself flows in my veins. My body is made from the same stuff as the stars. When I stare at the night sky, I see myself up there. When I look into myself, I see the universe. When my mind flows, it is nature itself flowing.

Experiences are full of pain and full of joy; this is simply in the nature of things. Since I am part of nature, I take part in everything it does. I cannot carve out what I don't like; that would be just the perspective of a transient form. Rather, I must take on the perspective of reality itself. I must use the creativity and freedom that nature reveals and maintain my mind in harmony with it. When I examine the things around and see what they are made of, the larger form they compose and the universal whole of which they are in turn only a smaller part, I can see their true nature and mine. When I see that, it becomes silly to want to change them. How can I change what is already infinite? I'm like a child splashing in the waves, trying to turn back the tide.

When I don't impose differences on things, when I analyze each according to its role in the larger process, I can discover that even the things that seem disgusting to me have equal value in nature. How presumptuous of me to think that I can improve on something so far beyond me. Reality is like a silken sheet, crumpling in on itself, folding and unfolding. Should I try to straighten out a crease?

My mind has the ability to move matter and to form thoughts and emotions. And I see this as the divine ability of nature moving itself. When I make my mind pure and quiet, I move from the mixture of pleasure and pain of daily life to the simple joy of existing. Understanding of nature brings tranquility, peace, and delight. When I consume what is dead I make it alive. When I eat, I take simple matter and rebuild myself with it, joining it to my own thoughts and emotions, into my own pleasure and pain. I marvel at the miracle of it all. What does this tell me of the nature of matter? How do I have the power to turn death into life; to turn dirt into experiences?

If I fear what is not to be feared or desire what is not to be desired, my mind will be troubled. This is my normal state of affairs as I move about in the world. But by examining nature, by examining myself, by purifying my thoughts and desires I can appreciate the things around me and love them uncluttered by my fears or desires. I can love them for their own true nature, not the layers of emotions and interpretations I impose on them. All of this can be seen in the present moment. I have no need of the past or future. The present moment is finite and because of that it has infinite value. In it is everything, all time, all space, all existence, all experience.

Everything is Full of Gods

Our world is one of tears, of joy and pain. Mind or intelligence is the pervasive ground of the universe, the foundation of existence. Reality is so strange. Anyone who claims to understand the world is either delusional or exaggerates or lies to themselves. Truth comes in glimpses and flashes. When those moments disappear, we are left with our inadequate thoughts and concepts, waving our hands, trying desperately to describe small pieces of what surrounds us. Reality transcends our understanding, no matter how hard we try. We are in the odd position of being neither completely ignorant of the truth nor able to fully comprehend it.

The nature of things is mysterious. We perceive its physical nature and we experience its mental nature. From this fundamental being, everything is composed. The nature of matter is to have mass and mind, extension and emotion, physicality and feeling. Although this nature surrounds us, although *it is us and we are it,* it remains an enigma. Nature is action, it is growth and decay, change and transformation, folding and unfolding into itself, creating within itself all possibility and all life. This cosmos fills each of us. In my own nature I can see the nature of all things, reflected back at me. Inside myself I can stare at the universe. It is the fabric of my being, the very stuff out of which I am made. The vortex of my self swirls in space-time, curling the universe into my human form, bending matter into my fleeting thoughts.

Many have come before me and many will come after. It is in the nature of things that they do not remain. The intense feeling I have of existing, the acute sensation of experience, will disappear someday. I know that. While I am here, however, I must decide how to live. I cannot waste these moments; all too soon, they will slip away and dissolve back into the ground of creation.

I am matter and I move myself, but at the same time matter moves all around me. This movement causes emotions and thoughts to arise in me, partly of my own doing and partly the doing of the external world. I must balance these movements, taking advantage of my own freedom to influence the world and simultaneously welcoming the world's action on me. I live in this tension between my exertions and the force of the world upon me. This is where the beauty of human relationships lies, in the harmony between my communication with someone and their communication back to me. If I allow the baser pleasures to take hold of me and cloud my mind, I will obscure the real beauty that surrounds me. The radiant wonder of the universe will be blurred and hidden as my mind obsesses over trivial things. Life is a struggle; but in that struggle comes fulfillment. In that trial comes stillness, when my understanding pierces the veil of nature it breaks free of my small and temporary form to fuse itself back into the universal being, back into the All. When I develop my awareness and achieve a deeper understanding of my own nature, I can see myself in all things and all things in me.

Spiritual Exercises

Because mind is an important feature of reality, mastering your mind is key to a happy life. You must understand your thoughts and integrate your emotions in order to see through to the true nature of things and to live serenely. Understanding will lead to tranquility.

In order to achieve this, you must exercise your mind. Contemplation is the exercise of reason. Just as physical exercises are important to maintain a healthy body, spiritual exercises are important to maintain a healthy mind (or soul).

As a type of training, spiritual exercises change your perspective. You see things as if for the first time. You will probably need to try many different exercises until you find one that resonates with you. Some people like to pray or worship, some like to meditate, others like to chant or dance. I have always found the exercise of reason—exploring the world with my mind—to be the most effective. It is a form of active meditation, turning a concept over and over in my mind until it becomes deeply ingrained in me.

Examples of spiritual exercises include: dialogue with oneself, examination of conscience, active or intentional imagination, reading inspiring books, writing down your thoughts, walking in nature, and daily disciplines such as resisting the swells of emotion that can lead to actions you might later regret.

For example, studying the works of ancient commentators and historians serve as windows into a world that has disappeared—vividly reminding us that everything fades away.

As another example, let's say you take a walk through a forest. The key is not to simply walk and let your mind wander, but to observe yourself walking, observe your thoughts and examine the things around you. Take them apart and put them back together in your mind. See what they are made of, where they come from and where they will go. See the surge of atoms with your mind's eye and see into the true nature of what surrounds you.

Or do the same with an old portrait. Don't just stare at the portrait; reflect on it. What did the subject see when she sat herself down to be painted? What kind of world surrounded her—sights, smells, physical sensations? What was going through her mind? Did she think that centuries later someone so distant would be staring at her image, wondering what her world was like? You have to take yourself out of your daily life, away from your common worries and struggles. You don't have to completely withdraw from the world, become a hermit in a cave or a stylite perched atop a pillar. In the midst of everyday activities, you can learn to turn inward—for example, by feeling the rise and fall of your breath or by observing the rising and falling of your thoughts and emotions.

Withdrawing your attention from the world and, instead, focusing on your thoughts, will reveal a rich inner world, full of surprises and insights. Those who dedicate themselves to long-term mindfulness (for example, monks) not only tend to achieve greater peace of mind but also enrich relationships with those they meet and interact with. As valuable as mindfulness and self-observation are—withdrawing attention from the external world—remaining engaged in the world, of course, is also worthy and valuable.

Work hard, get married, have children, and deal with all the struggles life entails. If you avoid the world, how can you know what's real? You cannot discover the truth about life by hiding from it; only by embracing it.

In the following pages, I repeat many of the concepts I explained earlier. This is one of the active meditations I do most often: contemplation of a certain philosophical concept.

As you contemplate the ideas and suggestions presented here, remain aware of the reality of the present moment—observe your thoughts and feel every feeling. Don't allow your feelings to fade away to nothing; instead fully experience them and use them to sharpen your mind and enrich your experiences.

Reality is not made of static things, but flowing processes. Everything consists of processes—everything flows. Yet everything is a just a ripple of the one true process: the universe itself. The universe continuously evolves and folds in on itself, wrinkling and furrowing the fabric of reality, cascading and splashing at every twist and turn.

Reality is a single flow, forever folding and unfolding, gushing with activity.

Everything is in constant motion. Activity never stops, the universe never stands still.

Look around you and see the flow. Peer inside the smallest particle; gaze up at the largest galaxy. Look inside yourself, and feel the flow of your mind. The entire ever-changing universe mirrors your ever-changing thoughts.

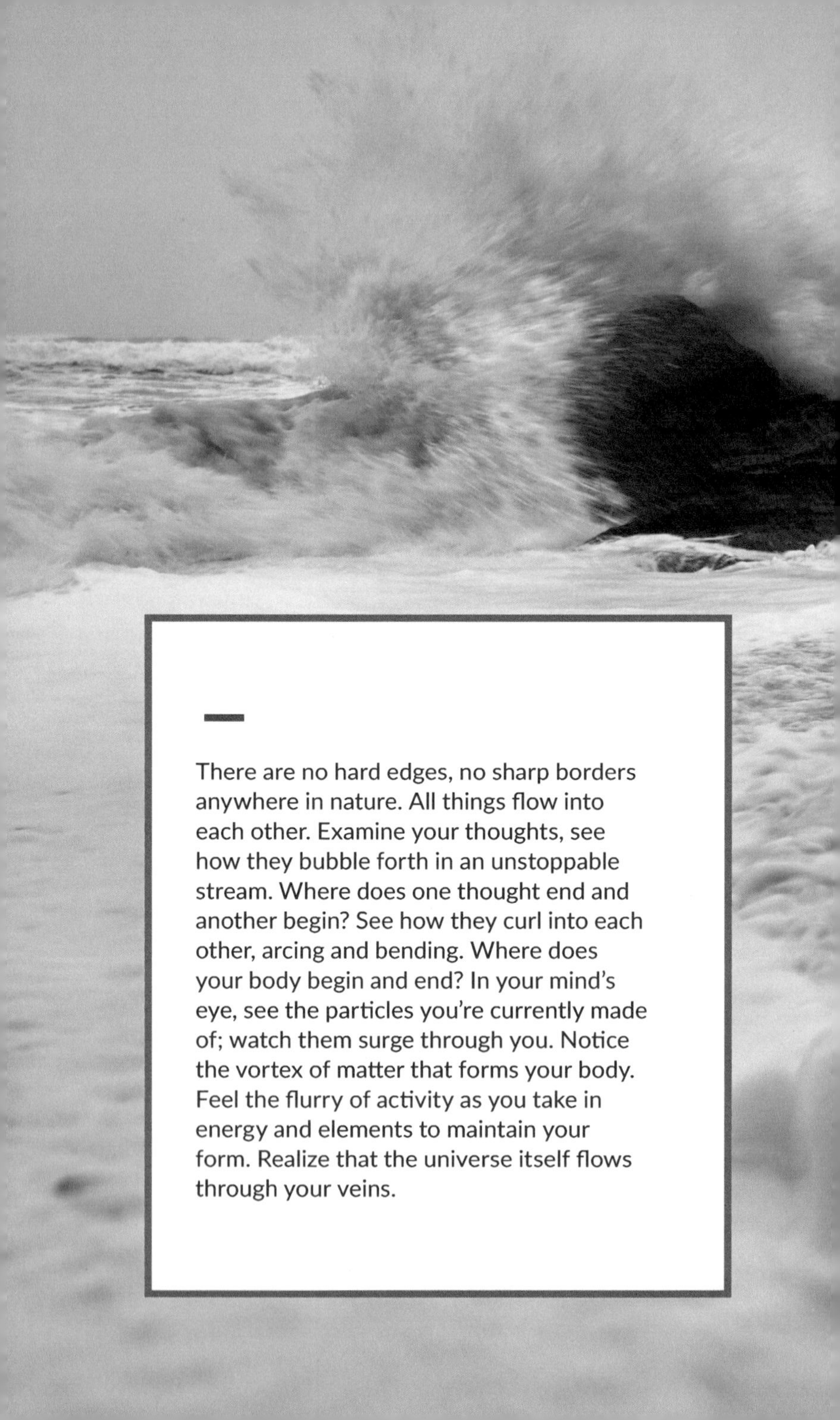

There are no hard edges, no sharp borders anywhere in nature. All things flow into each other. Examine your thoughts, see how they bubble forth in an unstoppable stream. Where does one thought end and another begin? See how they curl into each other, arcing and bending. Where does your body begin and end? In your mind's eye, see the particles you're currently made of; watch them surge through you. Notice the vortex of matter that forms your body. Feel the flurry of activity as you take in energy and elements to maintain your form. Realize that the universe itself flows through your veins.

The flow is everywhere you look

Concentrate on the present. See the world as if for the first and last time. Feel the flow inside yourself. Stay present to your experience right now—at this moment. Right now, you have access to all that exists.

Examine your stream of experience; observe your thoughts. Trace them back to their source, where they sprung from, and how they join with all things in the universal flux.

The churning clouds outside your mind reflect the frothing activity of your thoughts. Like a cauldron of creation, the universe bubbles and boils over, forever transforming itself. This is your nature.

A whirlwind of activity churns inside every cell. Molecules dance, vibrating with energy, surging along with the universal flow.

Every cell in your body contains the same sea water you evolved from. Molecules of all shapes and sizes continuously swirl in your cellular water, bouncing around and jostling each other, fitting together like pieces of a dynamic jigsaw to perform some task, then separate when it is done. As molecules break down, they are replaced from the atoms streaming all around them.

Even here the process continues. Nothing stays still; everything goes through motion, collision, decay, and regeneration.

Molecules flow in and out of our porous cells. Beneath our molecules, our atoms consist of roiling bundles of energy and clouds of electrons. These ever-flowing and streaming processes fold in on themselves, twisting and turning, and then unfolding and blossoming out. Contemplate the mystery of how all this physical, embodied activity shows up as experiences and sensations in your mind.

Look inside at all the activity: billions and billions of molecules pirouette and cascade through your body, affecting your emotions and sensations, accompanying your feeling of being alive, your experience of *being*.

Everything in the universe is fundamentally the same. What is the difference between the smallest bacteria and the largest mountain? Only the speed of the flow.

Nature exists and flows all around me. I melt into it. My body continuously rejoins the undulating matter that surrounds me, taking it in and exuding it out. I coalesce temporarily from the stuff of the universe and then soon disperse and fuse back into it.

The self is a vortex: matter flows through me, atoms from all over the world find their way into my body, forming me, and then flowing back out.

From small to large, everything participates in the same universal process. Examine the growth of moss and the miniature landscape it creates—a microcosm of the largest expanse of wilderness.

If you could watch the landscape of mountains and valleys form in a time-lapse video spanning thousands of years, would it look any different from the growth of mold? The scales are different, but fundamentally both are the same. The timespans vary, the spaces differ, but these are both the same pulsating reality.

Is the mold alive? Is the mountain?

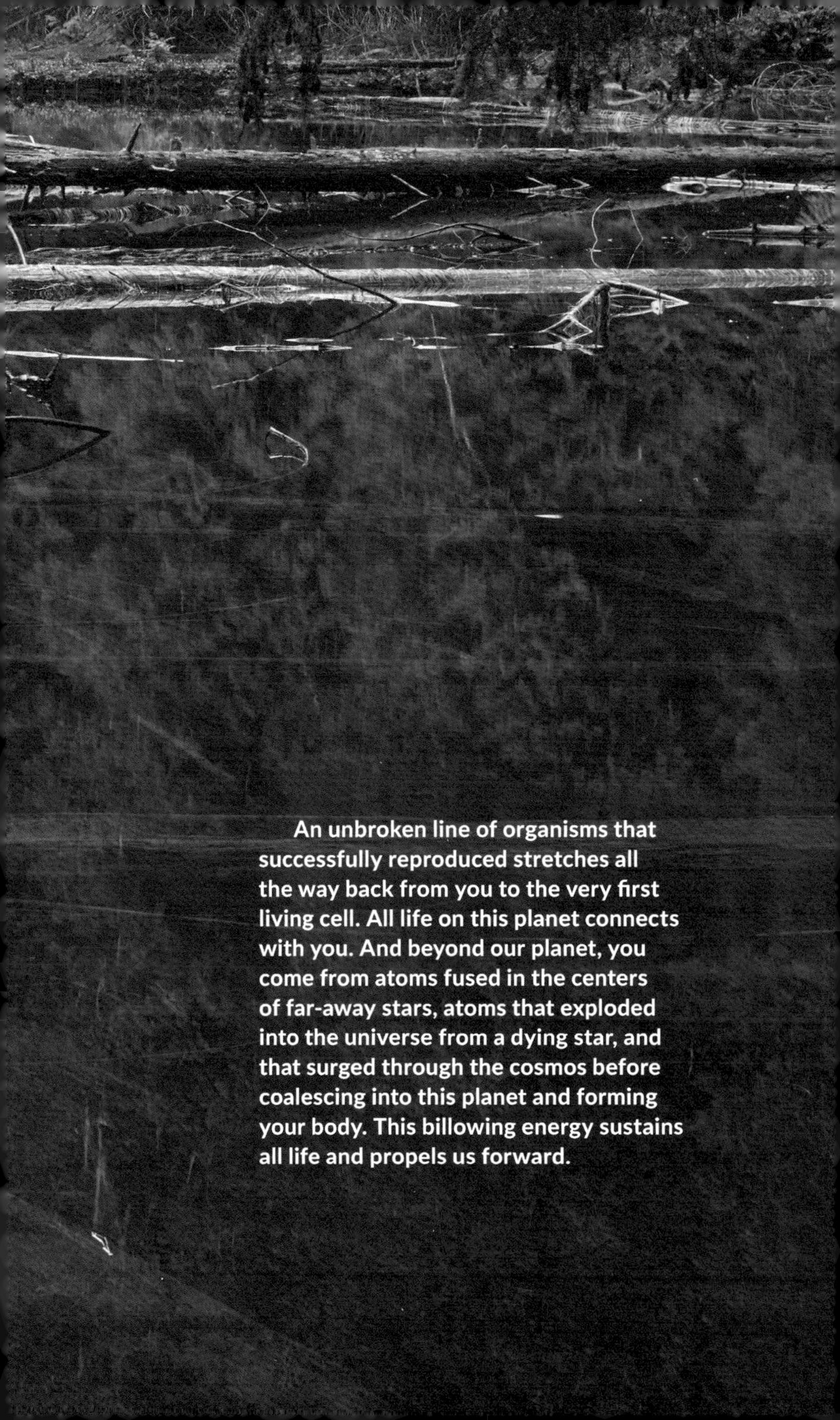

An unbroken line of organisms that successfully reproduced stretches all the way back from you to the very first living cell. All life on this planet connects with you. And beyond our planet, you come from atoms fused in the centers of far-away stars, atoms that exploded into the universe from a dying star, and that surged through the cosmos before coalescing into this planet and forming your body. This billowing energy sustains all life and propels us forward.

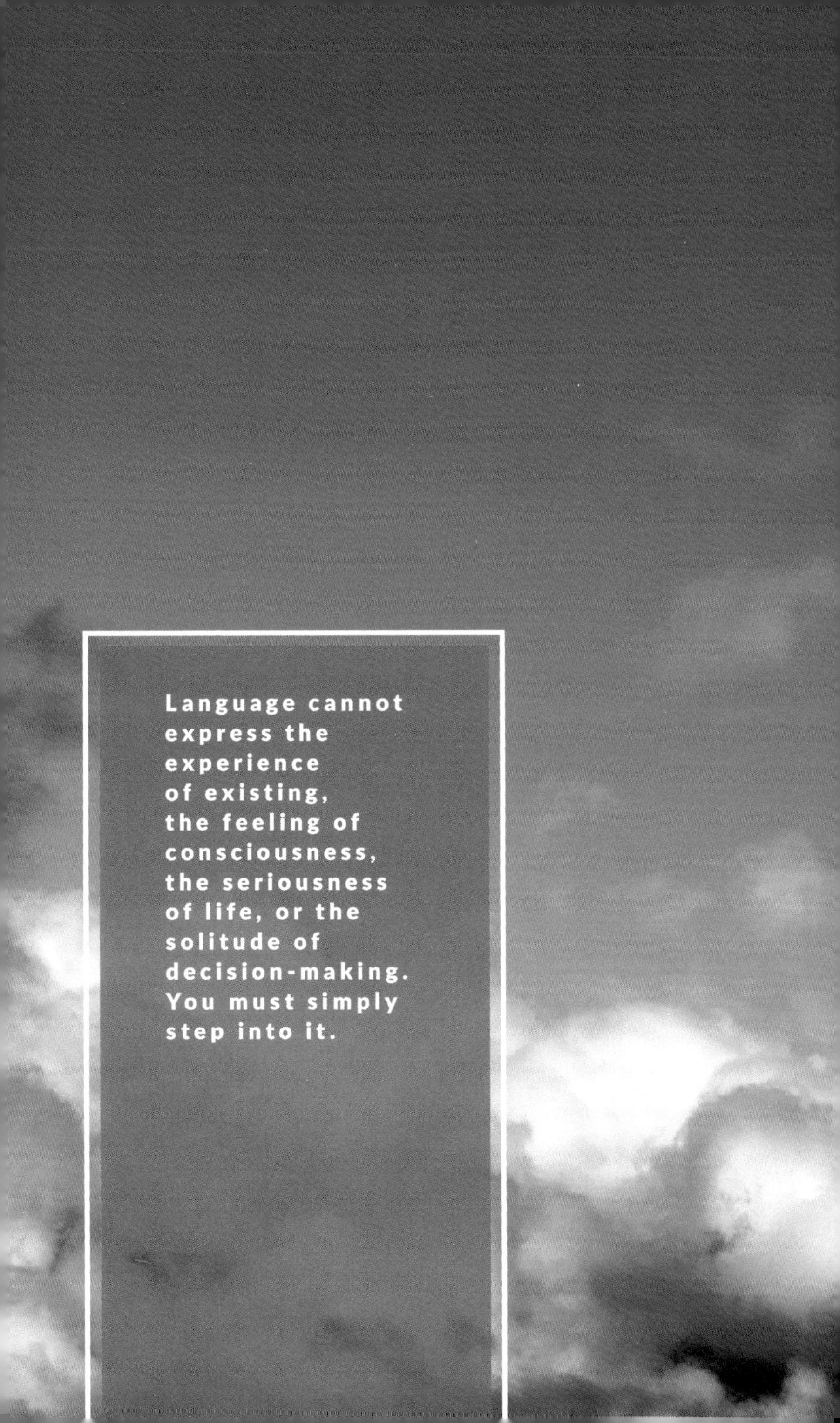

Language cannot express the experience of existing, the feeling of consciousness, the seriousness of life, or the solitude of decision-making. You must simply step into it.

Do not be tormented by desires for wealth, glory, power, and sensual pleasures. None of these can be satisfied in the present. These feelings are natural, let them come and let them go, but don't hold on. Desires always lead to more desires, blinding you to the present as you hunger for the future. By letting go of your desires, you can experience true pleasure and satisfaction.

When you let go of foolish cravings, when you see only the true nature of things, your mind radiates tranquility.

Look at all of the societies that have passed, all of the billions of people that have lived and died, and those that still remain. Time consumes everything. Nature is unceasing and restless. This is your fate.

The flow absorbs everything

Everything will be washed away, everything you see will soon be gone. Why should you try to hold on so tightly? How can you attach value to any of this?

Do not be disturbed by impermanence. Nothing can disturb your mind except if you let it. Rather, relax into the preciousness of this moment. Feel it.

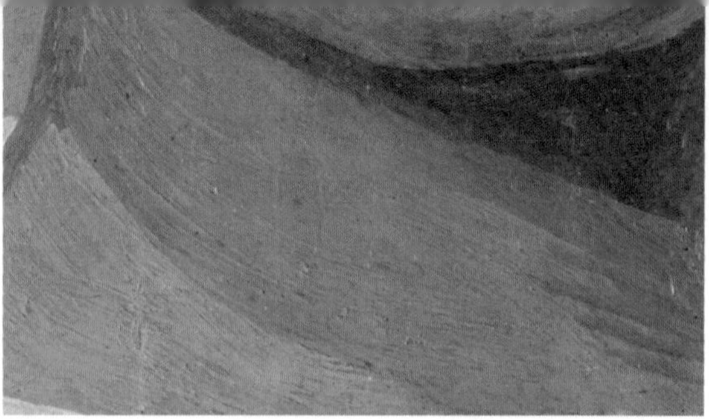

This is the mummy portrait of Eutyches who lived in second century AD, a Roman citizen in Egypt. While he lived, his experiences must have seemed so real. To him, reality was the buildings and people, the smells and sounds, the sights and sensations that enveloped him every day. All of that is gone now, his entire world and everyone he knew has disappeared, faded away, vanished and replaced. All that is left are dust and fragments. Would he have really believed, deep in his heart, that everything around him would dissolve? That everything would crumble? That everything would decay and regenerate many times over?

Look around at everything that surrounds you. Like a tide, reality surges passed you, a river rushing through you. Everything you see will grow, decay, and transform into something else. We live only in the present moment; the rest is lost behind us or lies still ahead and may never be reached.

Isn't it silly to care about what others think of you? To crave riches and fame? To think about anything other than what is real and in front of you?

If you have a normal lifespan, you will get 2.5 billion heartbeats. Feel each one as it comes and goes, know that it will not be replaced. What will you do with the heartbeats you have left?

Every single thing contains within it the seed of the entire universe. Because it is finite and fleeting, every moment has infinite value. Nothing lasts. Everything slips through your fingers. Nothing stands still for you to hold on to. But every moment is also the seed from which everything is created. Everything fades away, creating an opening for new experiences, new sensations, new life.

Because reality is transitory and ephemeral, it is also forever new. If it were static and unchanging, what would you be able to experience? The nature of things is, indeed, bittersweet.

You feel your pain, and you know suffering is real. But that is not all there is. As you feel pain, focus your reason. Comfort dulls the mind, but struggle sharpens it. Your mind is a citadel, strengthen it and you can withstand anything.

Your mind is a rock against which waves of emotion crash and break. You must not break with them; rather let them wash away whatever veils your understanding. Observe your thoughts, feel every feeling at every moment—both positive and negative. You decide what's good or bad by how you judge and react.

You may be proud of what you've accomplished, but what is that compared to the laws of nature? What have you contributed compared to the universal reason that guides everything? For you to achieve anything, photosynthesis must continue to produce oxygen, electrons must continue to have their same charge, and gravity must continue to have its same strength. How small a role you play in all of this.

What place is there for pride when faced with the awe-inspiring universal flow that surrounds you?

Mathematical structures exist independently of your mind, yet your mind can interact with them. They are not physical, they do not have spatial dimensions, they do not exist in time, yet they are true and eternal.
Their truth is not dependent on the thoughts of a particular mind. They describe the physical world perfectly. Can this be a coincidence? What is this world of mathematical truth that transcends physical objects, yet somehow describes all physical things? Matter and math are one. Contemplate the mystery of their unity.

We can imagine a universe where gravity has a different strength, but can you imagine a universe where 2 + 2 does not equal 4? These mathematical structures are not inventions of the human mind, like a human language. They have their own objective reality, existing long before human minds evolved, and will exist long after we are gone. Where does the truth of numbers come from? What gives them their reality? What can you do but wonder?

Everything you say about reality is false. All thoughts cloud your mind. You cannot capture what is true in words any more than you can catch mist with your hands. Explore the truth, but above all feel it.

Feel yourself flow through time. How many days can you remember? How many moments have already slipped past? Who remembers those moments now? Are they lost forever?

Your thoughts are ripples in the structure of reality. They form like waves on the surface of the ocean, then dissolve back into everything else. Your emotions are the froth of the fabric of nature, whitecaps forming on the crests, blowing away, then melting back into the mist that everything is made of.

The things around you are like bubbles, fragile, transitory, ready to burst at any moment and disappear. Enjoy them while they're here.

What is "red"? Particles of light bounce off an object and hit your eyes. Molecules in your eye change shape when the photons of light strikes them, triggering a cascade of electrochemical signals that surges to your brain—and then you see "red."

But photons are not "red," they merely move with a particular wavelength. The surface of a tomato isn't red; it just reflects a certain wavelength. The molecules in your eyes are not red, either. They are sensitive to light of different wavelengths because of changes in their chemical bonds, not because some are "red."

Those electrochemical signals are colorless. The optic nerve simply transmits pulses of information to your brain via electrically charged particles, the same signals that transmit information about vision, hearing, touch, and smell.

So what then is "red"? Where is the "red"?

Color, like other sensations, exists only in your mind.

Surrounded by clues, you already have everything you need to see the truth right there in front of you. Existence is one; reality is one; consciousness is one. You are a knot in the mind and body of the universe. Your mind can see the greater Mind that it is a part of. Abstract objects, mathematical structures, all exist as part of this one consciousness.

You recognize minds of a similar complexity to your own. But could you recognize more complex minds or less complex minds? Just because you can't recognize them, doesn't mean other kinds of minds don't exist.

When something tastes sweet, where is that sweetness? Is it in the molecules of fruit or in the molecules of your neurons? Are the molecules of your tongue sweet? What about the nerves that connect your tongue to your brain? None of these objects are sweet, yet you experience sweetness in your mind. How can you generate a sensation of sweetness from things that appear so different from it? Can those molecules and that sensation really be that different? What do they share in common?

From the outside we see light as wavelengths and vibrations. From the inside, light feels itself as pulses of emotion.

Nature is one thing. All life evolved from same source, all matter is composed atoms, and atoms are the same everywhere. Large or small, everything is ultimately the same. Examine time for a moment or for an eternity, it is the same. This is what you are made of.

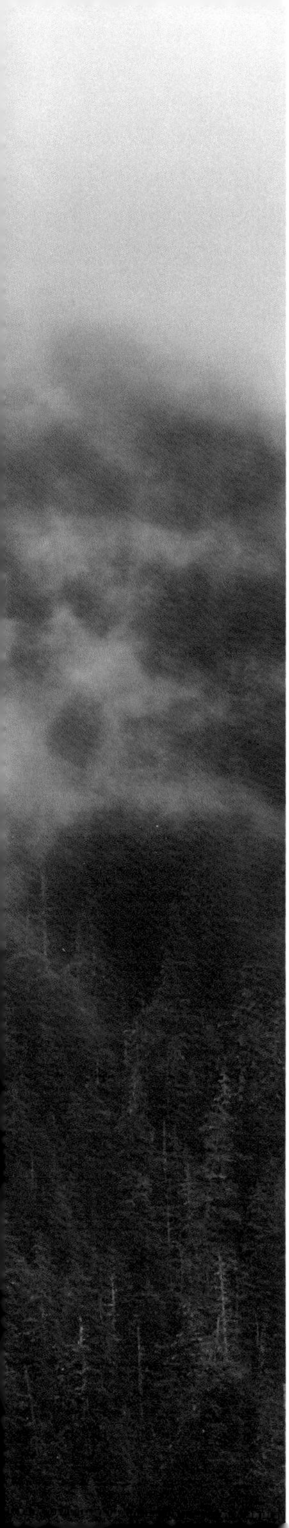

The things of nature can appear to us as stable and enduring.

But inside all things, billions of energetic individuals pulse with activity, flowing into and out of each other

Look inside yourself and see the matter flowing through you, like the buds of perception that form your thoughts.

These particles were once dispersed all over the world, now you have absorbed them into your body for a short time, before they flow back out to rejoin the rest of nature.

The most direct way to observe nature is through yourself, to observe it working in yourself, as it influences your own experience. Through the curiosity of your mind the universe see itself and understands itself

Bibliography

Alberts, Bruce. Molecular Biology of the Cell. New York: Garland Science, 2002. Print.

Aurelius, Marcus, and Gregory Hays. Meditations. New York: Modern Library, 2002. Print.

Aurelius, Marcus, C. Scot Hicks, and David V. Hicks. The Emperor's Handbook: A New Translation of The Meditations. New York: Scribner, 2002. Print.

Aurelius, Marcus, Jacob Needleman, and John P. Piazza. The Essential Marcus Aurelius. New York: Jeremy P. Tarcher/Penguin, 2008. Print.

Aurelius, Meditations, and Gregory Hays. Marcus Aurelius Meditations. Toronto: Random House, 2002. Print.

Baars, Bernard J., and Nicole M. Gage. Cognition, Brain, and Consciousness: Introduction to Cognitive Neuroscience. Amsterdam: Academic, 2007. Print.

Barrett, Louise, R. I. M. Dunbar, and John Lycett. Human Evolutionary Psychology. Princeton, NJ: Princeton UP, 2002. Print.

Boyer, Pascal. Religion Explained: The Evolutionary Origins of Religious Thought. New York: Basic, 2001. Print.

Braitenberg, Valentino. Vehicles, Experiments in Synthetic Psychology. Cambridge, MA: MIT, 1984. Print.

Bray, Dennis. Wetware: A Computer in Every Living Cell. New Haven: Yale UP, 2009. Print.

Campbell, Robin. Seneca: Letters from a Stoic. Middlesex: Penguin, 1969. Print.

Carroll, Sean B. Endless Forms Most Beautiful: The New Science of Evo Devo and the Making of the Animal Kingdom. New York: Norton, 2005. Print.

Carus, Titus Lucretius, and R. E. Latham. Lucretius on the Nature of the Universe. Harmondsworth, Middlesex: Penguin, 1958. Print.

Colyvan, Mark. The Indispensability of Mathematics. New York: Oxford UP, 2001. Print.

Cottingham, W. N., and D. A. Greenwood. An Introduction to the Standard Model of Particle Physics. Cambridge: Cambridge UP, 1998. Print.

Dennett, D. C. Freedom Evolves. New York: Viking, 2003. Print.

Desmond, William D. Cynics. Berkeley: U of California, 2008. Print.

Eddington, Arthur Stanley. The Nature of the Physical World. New York: Macmillan, 1928. Print.

Edelman, Gerald M. Second Nature: Brain Science and Human Knowledge. New Haven: Yale UP, 2006. Print.

Edelman, Gerald M. Wider than the Sky: The Phenomenal Gift of Consciousness. New Haven: Yale UP, 2004. Print.

Epictetus, and George Long. Enchiridion. Amherst, NY: Prometheus, 1991. Print.

Epictetus, and Robert F. Dobbin. Discourses and Selected Writings. London: Penguin, 2008. Print.

Epicurus, Brad Inwood, and Lloyd P. Gerson. The Epicurus Reader: Selected Writings and Testimonia. Indianapolis: Hackett, 1994. Print.

Fleming, Ursula, and Eckhart. Meister Eckhart: The Man from Whom God Hid Nothing. N.p.: Collins, 1988. Print.

Frank, Robert H. Passions within Reason: The Strategic Role of the Emotions. New York: Norton, 1988. Print.

Freeman, Kathleen. Ancilla to the Presocratic Philosophers: A Complete Translation of the Fragments in Diels, Fragmente Der Vorsokratiker. Oxford: Basil Blackwell, 1947. Print.

Freeman, Walter J. How Brains Make up Their Minds. New York: Columbia UP, 2000. Print.

Fuster, Joaquin M. Cortex and Mind: Unifying Cognition. Oxford: Oxford UP, 2003. Print.

Fuster, Joaquin M. The Prefrontal Cortex. London: Academic/ Elsevier, 2008. Print.

Gilbert, Scott F. Developmental Biology. Sunderland, MA: Sinauer, 2006. Print.

Goodsell, David S. The Machinery of Life. New York: Springer-Verlag, 1993. Print.

Gowers, Timothy, June Barrow-Green, and Imre Leader. The Princeton Companion to Mathematics. Princeton, NJ: Princeton UP, 2008. Print.

Griffin, David Ray. Unsnarling the World-knot: Consciousness, Freedom, and the Mind-body Problem. Berkeley, CA: U of California, 1998. Print.

Hadot, Pierre, Arnold I. Davidson, and Michael Chase. Philosophy as a Way of Life: Spiritual Exercises from Socrates to Foucault. Malden, MA: Blackwell, 1995. Print.

Hadot, Pierre, Marc Djaballah, Jeannie Carlier, and Arnold I. Davidson. The Present Alone Is Our Happiness: Conversations with Jeannie Carlier and Arnold I. Davidson. Stanford, CA: Stanford UP, 2009. Print.

Hadot, Pierre, Michael Chase, and Marcus Aurelius. The Inner Citadel: The Meditations of Marcus Aurelius. Cambridge, MA: Harvard UP, 1998. Print.

Hofstadter, Douglas R., and Daniel C. Dennett. The Minds I: Fantasies and Reflections of Self and Soul. Toronto: Bantam, 1988. Print.

Hölldobler, Bert, Edward O. Wilson, and Margaret Cecile Nelson. The Superorganism: The Beauty, Elegance, and Strangeness of Insect Societies. New York: W.W. Norton, 2009. Print.

Hunt, Arthur S. Selected Papyri. Cambridge, MA: Harvard UP, 1950. Print.

Huxley, Aldous. The Perennial Philosophy. New York: Harper & Brothers, 1945. Print.

Jaspers, Karl, and Hannah Arendt. Socrates, Buddha, Confucius, Jesus: The Paradigmatic Individuals. San Diego: Harcourt, Brace, Jovanovich, 1985. Print.

Jaspers, Karl, Hannah Arendt, and Ralph Manheim. Plato and Augustine. New York: Harcourt, Brace & World, 1962. Print.

Jaspers, Karl, Michael Ermarth, and Leonard H. Ehrlich. The Great Philosophers. New York: Harcourt Brace, 1995. Print.

Jaspers, Karl. Spinoza. New York: Harcourt Brace Jovanovich, 1974. Print.

Joyce, Richard. The Evolution of Morality. Cambridge, MA: MIT, 2006. Print.

Kauffman, Stuart A. At Home in the Universe: The Search for Laws of Self-organization and Complexity. New York: Oxford UP, 1995.

Print.

Kauffman, Stuart A. The Origins of Order: Self-organization and Selection in Evolution. New York: Oxford UP, 1993. Print.

Kauffman, Stuart A. Reinventing the Sacred: A New View of Science, Reason and Religion. New York: Basic, 2008. Print.

Kim, Jaegwon. Philosophy of Mind. Boulder, Col.: Westview, 1996. Print.

Laertius, Diogenes, and Robert Drew. Hicks. Lives of Eminent Philosophers: In Two Volumes. Cambridge (Mass.): Harvard UP, 1980. Print.

Lane, Nick. Power, Sex, Suicide: Mitochondria and the Meaning of Life. Oxford: Oxford UP, 2005. Print.

Lange, Marc. Philosophy of Science: An Anthology. Malden, MA: Blackwell Pub., 2007. Print.

Laurent. The Practice of the Presence of God: Conversations and Letters of Brother Lawrence. Oxford: Oneworld, 1999. Print.

Long, A. A. Epictetus: A Stoic and Socratic Guide to Life. Oxford: Clarendon, 2002. Print.

Maddy, Penelope. Naturalism in Mathematics. Oxford: Clarendon, 1997. Print.

Mason, Andrew S. Plato. Berkeley, CA: U of California, 2010. Print.

McLaughlin, Brian P., and Jonathan D. Cohen. Contemporary Debates in Philosophy of Mind. Malden, MA: Blackwell Pub., 2007. Print.

Merton, Thomas. New Seeds of Contemplation. Shatin, Hong Kong: Logos, 2002. Print.

Nadler, Steven M. Spinoza's Ethics: An Introduction. New York: Cambridge UP, 2006. Print.

Nagel, Thomas. Mind and Cosmos: Why the Materialist Neo-Darwinian Conception of Nature Is Almost Certainly False. New York: Oxford UP, 2012. Print.

Navia, Luis E. Diogenes the Cynic: The War against the World. Amherst, NY: Humanity, 2005. Print.

Navia, Luis E. Socrates: A Life Examined. Amherst, NY: Prometheus, 2007. Print.

O'Keefe, Tim. Epicureanism. Berkeley: U of California, 2010. Print.

Penrose, Roger. The Road to Reality: A Complete Guide to the Laws of the Universe. New York: A.A. Knopf, 2005. Print.

Plato, and Harold North Fowler. Euthyphro, Apology, Crito, Phaedo, Phaedrus. Cambridge, MA: Harvard UP, 1990. Print.

Remes, Pauliina. Neoplatonism. Berkeley: U of California, 2008. Print.

Rescher, Nicholas. Process Metaphysics: An Introduction to Process Philosophy. Albany: State U of New York, 1996. Print.

Rifkin, Benjamin A., and Michael J. Ackerman. Human Anatomy: From the Renaissance to the Digital Age. New York: Abrams, 2006. Print.

Rufus, C. Musonius, Cynthia Ann Kent King, and William Braxton Irvine. Musonius Rufus: Lectures & Sayings. United States: Createspace, 2011. Print.

Russell, Bertrand. Human Knowledge: Its Scope and Limits. New York: Simon and Schuster, 1948. Print.

Sagan, Carl, and Ann Druyan. The Varieties of Scientific Experience: A Personal View of the Search for God. New York: Penguin, 2006. Print.

Schoonover, Carl E. Portraits of the Mind: Visualizing the Brain from Antiquity to the 21st Century. New York: Abrams, 2010. Print.

Schopf, J. William. Life's Origin: The Beginnings of Biological Evolution. Berkeley: U of California, 2002. Print.

Sellars, John. The Art of Living: The Stoics on the Nature and Function of Philosophy. Aldershot, Hants, England: Ashgate, 2003. Print.

Sellars, John. Stoicism. Berkeley: U of California, 2006. Print.

Seneca, Lucius Annaeus, and C. D. N. Costa. On the Shortness of Life. New York: Penguin, 2005. Print.

Sherburne, Donald W. A Key to Whitehead's Process and Reality. New York: Macmillan, 1966. Print.

Sider, Theodore, John Hawthorne, and Dean W. Zimmerman. Contemporary Debates in Metaphysics. Malden, MA: Blackwell Pub., 2008. Print.

Skrbina, David. Panpsychism in the West. Cambridge, MA: MIT,

2005. Print.

Smith, John Maynard, and Eörs Szathmáry. The Major Transitions in Evolution. Oxford: W.H. Freeman Spektrum, 1995. Print.

Smith, John Maynard, and Eörs Szathmáry. The Origins of Life: From the Birth of Life to the Origin of Language. Oxford: Oxford UP, 1999. Print.

Smith, John Maynard. On Evolution: John Maynard Smith,. Edinburgh: U, 1972. Print.

Solé, Ricard V., and Brian C. Goodwin. Signs of Life: How Complexity Pervades Biology. New York: Basic, 2000. Print.

Spinoza, Benedictus De. On the Improvement of the Understanding. Champaign, IL: Project Gutenberg, 2001. Print.

Sporns, Olaf. Networks of the Brain. Cambridge, MA: MIT, 2011. Print.

Strawson, Galen, and Anthony Freeman. Consciousness and Its Place in Nature: Does Physicalism Entail Panpsychism? Exeter, UK: Imprint Academic, 2006. Print.

Stringer, Chris, and Peter Andrews. The Complete World of Human Evolution. London: Thames & Hudson, 2005. Print.

Suzuki, Shunryu, and Trudy Dixon. Zen Mind, Beginner's Mind. N.p.: n.p., 2005. Print.

Thompson, Evan. Mind in Life: Biology, Phenomenology, and the Sciences of Mind. Cambridge, MA: Belknap of Harvard UP, 2007. Print.

Varela, Francisco J., Evan Thompson, and Eleanor Rosch. The Embodied Mind: Cognitive Science and Human Experience. Cambridge, MA: MIT, 1991. Print.

Waal, F. B. M. De, Stephen Macedo, Josiah Ober, and Robert Wright. Primates and Philosophers: How Morality Evolved. Princeton, NJ: Princeton UP, 2006. Print.

White, Thomas I. In Defense of Dolphins: The New Moral Frontier. Malden, MA: Blackwell Pub., 2007. Print.

Wilczek, Frank. The Lightness of Being: Mass, Ether, and the Unification of Forces. New York, NY: Basic, 2008. Print.

Wolters, Clifton. The Cloud of Unknowing, and Other Works. Harmondsworth: Penguin, 1978. Print.